Praise for *Go Long*

"One of my fundamental beliefs as CEO is that prioritizing the short-term at the expense of the long-term is simply not sustainable and perpetuates the kinds of boom-splat cycles that aren't good for any business or stakeholder. That's why *Go Long* is a must-read. If you're looking to build or lead a company that grows consistently not just from quarter to quarter, but year to year, that balances short-term and long-term priorities, that focuses on both the level and duration of returns, this book is for you."
—Indra Nooyi, Chairman and CEO, PepsiCo, Inc.

"In Amgen's business of biotechnology, investments in significant innovations can begin up to a decade before we begin to see substantial returns. Through deep insights and original reporting, *Go Long* helps to bring leaders and investors the principles they need to keep long-term thinking at the heart of their strategies."
—Robert Bradway, Chairman and CEO, Amgen

"Intensifying demands for near-term corporate performance can force immediate gains but also lasting damage on company prospects and stakeholder fortunes. With inside accounts of how some of the world's leading business executives manage for the future, *Go Long* provides a tangible roadmap for long-term leadership. To improve the state of this world, here is a primer for doing so."
—Klaus Schwab, Founder and Executive Chairman,
 World Economic Forum, and author, *The Fourth Industrial*
 Revolution **and** *Shaping the Fourth Industrial Revolution*

"*Go Long* combines insightful analysis with inspiring stories to show CEOs, boards, and investors how purpose-driven strategies can create important economic and societal benefits."
—Rosabeth Moss Kanter, Harvard Business School Professor and
 Chair and Director, Harvard Advanced Leadership Initiative

"The toughest test of leadership is leaving an enterprise stronger in every sense when your tenure is done. *Go Long* reminds us that while short term priorities come and go, a leader can't achieve that objective without a North star of a committed long term strategy and vision."
—James McNerney, former Chairman and CEO, The Boeing Co.

"*Go Long* provides critical advice to corporate leaders dealing with today's most pressing issue of business strategy—long term versus short term management. Must reading for directors, CEOs and all executives."
—**Martin Lipton, a founding partner, Wachtell, Lipton, Rosen & Katz**

"*Go Long* sharply delineates the tradeoffs that executives face in setting priorities. Decisions that build long-term value are the essence of great leadership."
—**Donald J. Gogel, Chairman and CEO, Clayton, Dubilier & Rice**

FOREWORD BY DAVID M. RUBENSTEIN

GO LONG

WHY LONG-TERM THINKING
IS YOUR BEST SHORT-TERM STRATEGY

DENNIS CAREY
KORN FERRY

BRIAN DUMAINE
FORTUNE MAGAZINE

MICHAEL USEEM
THE WHARTON SCHOOL

RODNEY ZEMMEL
McKINSEY & COMPANY

Wharton
DIGITAL PRESS
Philadelphia

Published by Wharton Digital Press
The Wharton School
University of Pennsylvania
3620 Locust Walk
2000 Steinberg Hall-Dietrich Hall
Philadelphia, PA 19104
Email: whartondigitalpress@wharton.upenn.edu
Website: http://wdp.wharton.upenn.edu/

Ebook ISBN: 978-1-61363-089-1
Paperback ISBN: 978-1-61363-088-4

Contents

Foreword

David M. Rubenstein
Cofounder and co-executive chairman, The Carlyle Group

I n the 1960s, with the rapid-growing institutional and retail partici-
pation in public equity markets, much investor interest developed
in the short-term stock performance of public companies. Investors
were far less interested in holding on to AT&T or GM shares for a
generation and much more interested in moving in and out of stocks,
based on perceived or actual short-term earnings growth.

This phenomenon produced an exponential rise in the 1960s of
institutional public equities analysts covering every development
in a public company's performance. The popular investment trend
seemed largely to be one of moving frequently in and out of stocks.
Long-term holds were increasingly viewed as the province of bank
trust departments.

The phenomenon of seeking short-term gains grew even more
dramatically in the subsequent decades as much more money from
growing pension funds, IRAs, 401(k)s, and mutual funds flowed into
the institutional and retail equity markets.

For a great many investors, the focus was largely on the next
quarter's earnings (for that would affect the near-term stock price).
A long-term perspective was to focus on earnings two and three
quarters down the road, and that long-term perspective did not appeal
to many of those investors. Other than Warren Buffett and a few of
his followers, no one seemed to focus on what might happen 5 and
10 years down the road.

This relatively short-term focus on near-term earnings inevitably resulted in public company CEOs focusing their own attention on meeting short-term earnings expectations.

It could be argued that this interest in public companies' short-term performance was not wholly bad. Stock markets flourished, creating enormous levels of wealth for investors. The US economy dramatically expanded and blossomed, despite the inevitable recessions and crises that occurred during the 1960s through the turn of the century. Many new companies, aided by well-funded venture capitalists, were created and transformed industries. Older companies were reinvented and modernized, aided by private equity investors. And the American economy truly dominated the global economy in the last half of the twentieth century, in a way few economies had ever dominated the global economy.

But then came the twenty-first century. Existing competition from European and other developed economies intensified. The emerging markets (most particularly China) challenged American companies (and the US economy) as they had never before been challenged. And many well-known, old-line US companies that had focused on next quarter's earnings suddenly had fewer weapons to compete in the newer world. Continued American global dominance was not inevitable.

Fortunately for the US economy, a number of entrepreneurs (toward the end of the past century, but principally in the early part of this century) tried to reinvent the world a bit by focusing more on longer-term goals and less on next quarter's earnings. And these companies prospered in ways that those focused principally on the next quarter could not have anticipated. The best known of these longer-term-focused companies—Apple, Amazon, Facebook, Google, and Microsoft—overcame competitors focused on the short term.

These new companies typically sprang from the vision of a founder dedicated to building a better product or providing a better service, with little focus on short-term concerns. The focus was on 10 years down the road, not 10 weeks or even 10 months.

These founders—with the strength of their convictions and near-manic pursuit of longer-term growth and excellence—often gave short shrift to the concern of institutional analysts or investors about short-term earnings.

Perhaps most famously, the Wall Street herd derided Amazon's lack of concern about near-term quarterly earnings. Jeff Bezos, the company's CEO, was focused on long-term growth and essentially ignored analyst demands for short-term earnings.

The result is now well known. Amazon became one of the world's most valuable companies—and Bezos the world's richest man—in large part because of his focus on producing earnings not in the next quarter but 5, 10, and 20 years down the road.

While the US economy has no doubt benefited in this century from CEO-founders like Jeff Bezos, who are able to focus on the longer term, the truth is that most public company CEOs are not visionary founders. Rather, they are increasingly focused on next quarter's earnings. And the focus is becoming more intense than ever before for a variety of reasons:

- The tenure for most public company CEOs is shorter than in the past—and shorter tenure inevitably means CEOs tend to focus on shorter-term objectives.

- Hedge funds, with quite short-term investment goals, have increasingly become large investors in public company stocks—and they prompt these companies to also focus on the short term.

- Some of these hedge funds—along with other investment vehicles—are taking on the role of activist investors ("activist" is now often a euphemism for short-term investment goals).

- Well-capitalized, algorithm-based, computer-driven investors are growing in market importance and size, and their focus is inevitably toward serving short-term gains.

- Plaintiffs' lawyers are invariably focusing their attention on short-term earnings declines that may not have been anticipated by markets—few lawsuits are filed against public companies for failing to project sufficiently long-term earnings and corporate growth objectives.

- Regulatory oversight from federal and state governments also invariably focuses on short-term earnings surprises (more typically on the downside). Here, too, regulators do not penalize CEOs or companies for failing to have solid 5- and 10-year earnings growth plans.

The consequences of these more modern phenomena seem to be binary. CEOs of public companies are paying more attention than ever to the next quarter's earnings. Or, those CEOs who can control whether a company should go public are choosing to keep a company private for as long as possible so they can avoid the public company need to produce higher and higher quarterly earnings. (Today, although the number of companies in the United States is significantly higher than 20 years ago, the number of public companies is down by 50%, from roughly 7,300 to 3,600.)

Of course, every company does not have the opportunity to go or stay private. Those companies that are public often have little choice in remaining public, and thereby their CEOs are increasingly subjecting themselves to the just-described modern pressures to focus on the short term.

Why is this really a problem? Great companies prosper by focusing on longer-term objectives—by spending money on research and development and capital improvements. And economies (and thereby societies) prosper by having companies grow, innovate, and improve over longer periods rather than just next quarter.

A number of financial industry leaders have in recent years tried to point out the increasing dangers of short-termism to companies' and economies' futures. And they have succeeded in making the issue one that is appropriate for serious public dialogue. Unfortunately, the increasing public attention to the issue has to date had less measurable impact than might be desired.

Perhaps some incremental, and much needed, impact will be achieved by a serious look at some of the public company CEOs who, in the current short-term atmosphere, chose, at some financial risk to their companies (and themselves), to focus on the long term. They might well be viewed as the Corporate Profiles in Courage.

Four experienced business practitioners and scholars—Dennis Carey, Michael Useem, Rodney Zemmel, and Brian Dumaine—have in fact provided just such a serious look. In *Go Long*, they have provided a well-researched analysis of how six current-generation public company CEOs successfully ignored short-term concerns. The results in all of these cases were stronger companies and better contributors to the well-being of their employees, suppliers, customers, and shareholders.

For anyone who is concerned about the importance of forcing longer-term objectives into a public company short-term mindset, and who wants to learn more about some of the heroes of this effort, this book is a godsend. Indeed, it should be mandatory reading for the CEOs and boards of all public companies. And perhaps because of this book, and public conversations that might result, the tide will begin turning, even if slowly at first, as longer-term corporate goals replace shorter-term goals.

And if that is the case, the authors will have truly done a public service by showing public company CEOs that it is best to focus on long-term goals if they want to also achieve short-term goals. And if they want to build great and enduring companies.

Introduction

Every year the nation's top business leaders convene at the CEO Academy, a gathering originally founded by one of our co-authors, Dennis Carey, and now offered in collaboration with The Wharton School and McKinsey & Company. Many business ideas get bandied about at this off-the-record gathering in New York City, but the CEOs who have attended over the past couple of years seemed particularly fixated on one very important topic: managing for the long term. As it turns out, they aren't alone.

Top executives today are feeling squeezed by activist hedge funds and institutional investors who are constantly pressuring them to boost quarterly earnings, increase dividends, and buy back shares— all at the expense of future growth. A 2014 global survey of more than 600 C-suite executives and directors conducted by the non-profit Focusing Capitalism on the Long Term (FCLT) reported that two-thirds of those surveyed said pressure for short-term results had increased over the previous five years.[1] As a result, R&D budgets have been cut, new product launches delayed, and productive and creative people laid off.

The FCLT survey is just one more piece in a mountain of evidence that suggests many American investors are putting enormous pressure on CEOs to make a quick buck. Short-termism, it seems, is everywhere. According to the New York Stock Exchange,[2] the average holding period for public shares has dropped from 5.1 years in the mid-1970s to 7.3 *months* today. This is partly due to the rise of high-frequency programmed trading, but even some institutional investors are making short-term bets. After all, they have to answer to their *own* investors, who also demand robust short-term gains *now*.

Activist investors, too, are playing a critical role in this chase for quick money. In 2017, Nelson Peltz of Trian targeted Procter & Gamble, Barry Rosenstein of Jana Partners attacked Whole Foods, and Mantle Ridge's Paul Hilal went after the railroad CSX—just to name a few of the more notable activist investor attacks.[3] And while these activist hedge funds represent only about 1% of the equity market, their influence is outsized, as they have been able to accumulate massive war chests thanks to low interest rates and the banking sector's willingness to accept very high leverage ratios. As of 2015 this group in aggregate had $122 billion under management,[4] up from only about $2 billion in 2001.[5]

Sometimes activists can play an important and positive role in improving the performance of a lagging company, but more typically when they attack they are essentially saying that management and the board are not maximizing shareholder return *today*. They call for share buybacks, spin-offs, increased dividends, and board restructurings—all aimed at boosting shareholder returns in the short run. (Ironically, a study by McKinsey found that share repurchases seldom have any lasting positive effect on total shareholder return.)[6] These investors argue that they are following a standard capitalist formula—forcing managers to drive down costs and boost productivity, which ultimately leads to increasing levels of wealth.

It certainly doesn't help matters that the stock market has historically rewarded CEOs who return capital to investors through dividends and stock buybacks—rough proxies for short-term strategies that keep investors happy. Goldman Sachs found that since 1991 those S&P stocks offering the highest combined dividend and share-buyback yields have returned an annualized 15.5%.[7] That's a higher rate of return than that of the S&P 500 index in total and also, unfortunately, outpaces the returns generated by a number of forward-thinking companies that invested in their future through R&D and other capital expenditures.

The good news is that there is growing evidence that long-term thinking pays in the long run. The McKinsey Global Institute examined the performance of 615 large- and mid-cap US publicly listed companies from 2001 to 2015, looking at patterns of investment, growth, earnings quality, and earnings management. This lens allowed McKinsey to separate long-term companies from others, and then compare their relative performance. Among its findings was that the revenue of long-term firms, which spent on average 50% more on R&D, cumulatively grew on average 47% more than that of the other firms, and with less volatility. Cumulatively, the earnings of long-term firms also grew 36% more on average.[8]

Not only did these long-term businesses increase profits, but they were also engines of job growth, adding nearly 12,000 more jobs on average than less-forward-thinking firms. The study concludes that had all US publicly listed firms created as many jobs as the long-term firms, the American economy would have added more than five million jobs—and another $1 trillion of GDP over the past decade.[9]

But what about that Goldman Sachs study? Well, although one year of performance does not constitute a trend—the situation might be starting to shift. In 2017, those companies in the Goldman study that spent more on capital expenditures and R&D outperformed those offering high dividends and buybacks by 11 percentage points.

We should note here that when it comes to short-termism there is plenty of blame to go around—and some of that blame can actually be traced to the C-suite. Yes, the investment community and meddlesome activists are certainly part of the problem, but the very same FCLT survey that revealed the increasing short-term pressures facing CEOs also found that nearly two-thirds of those CEOs said the pressure to deliver strong short-term financial performance stemmed from *their own board* and *their own executive team*. In other words, some of the short-term thinking we're seeing is actually self-imposed, with CEOs simply getting in their own way.

What makes the plague of short-term thinking somewhat puzzling is that, according to McKinsey estimates, 75% of the US market is held by buy-and-hold investors who are actually interested in the long-term value of the companies in which they've invested.[10] Given this, you could argue that CEOs shouldn't be putting so much pressure on themselves to get strong short-term results. At the very least, we posit that they certainly have the power—and, indeed, the obligation—to ignore some of that activist pressure and start thinking long term.

Yes, it's true that in the short term CEOs must still face fierce competition in their industry. And they must still live with the fear that if they don't deliver great returns in the short run, they too might soon become the target of activists. But it is our belief that they must never sell out the next decade in favor of next week. Indeed, as former GE CEO Jack Welch once explained: "You can't grow long-term if you can't eat short-term. Anybody can manage short. Anybody can manage long. Balancing those two things is what management is."[11]

As Welch understands, it is well within the power of all CEOs to find a happy balance between short-term performance and long-term growth. Getting this right is the ultimate responsibility of all CEOs—and that responsibility extends not only to their shareholders but also to their employees, their communities, and, indeed, the entire world.

Why You Should Read This Book

Rampant short-termism should be a concern to all of us because the stakes are so high. We believe that a strategy largely driven by short-term thinking, where the desire for quick profits mortgages the future of a business, is not sustainable and that the CEOs who engage in such behavior are doing damage to our economy and to society. In fact, we believe that the current short-sighted behaviors of many corporations—both real and the public's perception of it—are helping to erode support for capitalism itself.

Whether it is activist investors pushing for short-term profit taking at the expense of future growth, corporations paying workers below-market wages, CEOs engaging in convoluted strategies to avoid paying their fair share of taxes, or managers shirking their

environmental and worker safety obligations in pursuit of quick profits, these narrow and self-interested short-term behaviors are making many question the legitimacy and fairness of our free-market
system.

Little wonder that a 2017 survey by the American Culture and
Faith Institute found that 4 out of 10 American adults 18 years of age
and older prefer socialism to capitalism. The millennial generation
is even less enamored with America's economic system.[12] A 2016
Harvard study that polled young adults between the ages of 18 and
29 found that 58% of respondents do *not* support capitalism.[13]

If we are to preserve capitalism, capitalism will need to change.
As the prominent Wall Street lawyer Marty Lipton of Wachtell, Lipton,
Rosen & Katz puts it, there is a "New Paradigm" emerging where
corporations, their CEOs and boards of directors, leading institutional
investors, and asset managers all recognize that long-term thinking
is good for the economy, good for companies, good for shareholders,
and good for democracy. "This emerging consensus has reached a
tipping point," writes Lipton, "and decisive action is imperative."[14]

From our vantage point, we see—as Lipton does—too many
examples of CEOs wasting time and precious resources trying to
meet quarterly earnings, engaging in accounting stratagems, and cutting valuable people and projects to please a small group of influential investors on Wall Street. But we've also studied the best of the
best—those leaders who know how to run a business that thrives
not just for the benefit of shareholders but also for that of employees,
customers, and the communities in which they live. And those are
the accounts we'd like to share with you.

Today's CEOs need a roadmap to long-term management more
than ever before, and that's what we have set out to provide in this
book. We go behind the scenes to find out how some of the most successful business leaders of our time have navigated this treacherous
landscape. For our examples we focused mostly on US-based CEOs
because that's where the issue feels the most acute right now. But the
management wisdom offered here also applies to leaders and companies working around the globe.

We believe we're in a particularly good position to draw back the curtain and explain how top CEOs have pulled off this difficult balancing act. One of our coauthors, Michael Useem, a professor at The Wharton School of the University of Pennsylvania, has researched and written extensively about leadership and management. For two of his most recent books, *The India Way* and *Fortune Makers*, he and his coauthors interviewed Chinese and Indian CEOs and witnessed firsthand how they manage for the long term. As a vice chairman of the global executive search and talent management firm Korn Ferry, Dennis Carey has helped select dozens of directors and CEOs of Global Fortune 500 companies over the course of his career. He knows firsthand which qualities make for a business leader who knows how to manage for the long term. Rodney Zemmel, the managing partner of McKinsey's New York and Northeast offices in the United States, works closely with CEO clients who are striving to improve their long game and has deep knowledge of what works and what doesn't. Brian Dumaine, a *Fortune* magazine contributor, has covered the business world for three decades and has a journalist's perspective on what makes a leader succeed or fail.

In part one of the book we profile five CEOs and one director who have been able to resist today's rampant short-termism. Each has made bold moves that leveraged long-term thinking to win in the marketplace. What do they have in common? They invest heavily in their companies and in their people to create new opportunities and better-paying jobs. They balance the short-term needs of some investors with those of employees, customers, communities, and other stakeholders. Plus, they communicate to their boards, their executive teams, and their investors the idea that the very purpose of their business extends beyond short-term profits.

In the following pages you will learn how:

- CEO Alan Mulally had to make deep cuts and sell off businesses when he was turning around Ford, but he did it while investing boldly in new cars and technologies. To get his team to buy into this kind of radical change, he implemented a very hard-nosed financial formula for long-term growth called "profitable growth for all."

- Wall Street for the most part agreed with CVS Health CEO Larry Merlo's long-term strategy of becoming a retail healthcare company. It would not, however, have been the one to come up with the idea of how to go about it. He took an annual revenue hit of $2 billion by declaring his chain would no longer sell cigarettes. The move gave CVS credibility as it transitioned to its long-term strategy of becoming a true healthcare provider.

- When Unilever CEO Paul Polman came under attack from a private equity firm for investing too much in the future of this consumer goods company, he fought the firm off by being able to link the company's strong stock market performance to his long-term vision to build a sustainable corporation. Its mission? To help alleviate world poverty.

- Verizon CEO Ivan Seidenberg came under pressure by investors who wanted him to slash costs and sell off business. Instead, he invested $150 billion in the business and built two of the nation's largest wireless and broadband networks.

- After the financial crisis hit, 3M was a likely target for activists because of its lackluster growth and uninspired earnings. Faced with this challenge, CEO Sir George Buckley thought like an activist, found hundreds of millions in cash flow by reengineering the company's manufacturing logistics, and then used that money to boost R&D spending and unleash hundreds of new products.

- CEOs who want to go long need directors who get deeply involved in setting a strategy. Hewlett Packard Enterprise and Costco director Maggie Wilderotter tells how she and her fellow board members help CEOs to get the most out of their boards.

In part two, we offer operating principles for leaders who want to start thinking long term.

We hope that this book will act as a guide for executives, directors, and investors who want to learn about the value of long-term investing—and how it's done right. We believe that the CEOs profiled here offer valuable lessons for dealing with the quarterly pressures of Wall Street, fending off activist attacks, building a long-term strategy, and executing it with grace under fire.

As DowDuPont CEO Ed Breen puts it: "Focus on long-term value instead of fixating on short-term performance and share price. Make bets that are right for the institution—they should last longer than any CEO."[15]

Going long is not an easy task, but it can be done. And the stakes are too high not to try.

Part One
The Secrets of Leaders
Who Go Long

Chapter 1

Ford's $48 Billion Turnaround

While facing financial Armageddon, Ford CEO Alan Mulally kept a laser-like focus on where he wanted his company to be five years out. Ultimately, this helped him make smarter short-term decisions.

Everyone is going to benefit if you think of what you're doing as creating value for all.
—Alan Mulally, former CEO of the Ford Motor Co.
and Boeing Commercial Airplanes

When Alan Mulally arrived at the troubled Ford Motor Company in the fall of 2006 the situation was even worse than he had feared. The company's once-blue-chip stock was trading below $10 a share, its debt was headed toward junk territory, sales of its profitable SUVs and pickups in North America—staggered by a sudden rise in gas prices—were in a free fall, and the company's top brass, embroiled in savage infighting, had been unable to implement a strategy to spark a turnaround. And yet by the time Mulally left in 2014, he had raised Ford's stock market capitalization by $48 billion.[16] How did he do it? By focusing on the long term.

One of the toughest challenges any CEO faces is staying focused on a long-term strategy while having to deal with short-term distractions. Contentious earnings calls, a division whose sales are slipping, a product launch that's fallen behind, or a key manager who's demoralizing the troops—all these short-term crises can distract the best of CEOs and their team from driving home a long-term strategy.

By fixating too much on the short term, a CEO can end up adrift. Sears, for example, wrestled day by day to refurbish its stores and improve customer service in an age when customers were gravitating away from brick-and-mortar stores and shopping more online. By 2017 Sears's revenue and same-store sales continued to decline at a double-digit pace, and the company struggled to pay back its massive debt load. The point is that CEOs facing a crisis can easily become distracted by all the bush fires that they believe need extinguishing.

This could have been Mulally's fate. But from day one he had a long-term vision for Ford—one that he believed would guide it out of its crisis. In 2006, Bill Ford, the great-grandson of Henry and the previous CEO of the company, invited Mulally in to fix the organization. Ford stayed on as executive chairman and Mulally took over his role as CEO. Soon after arriving at corporate headquarters in Dearborn, Michigan, Mulally found that the situation was even worse than he had feared. He discovered that Ford was on track to lose $17 *billion* the coming year.

Most CEOs in that situation would take dramatic steps to staunch the short-term bleeding, and Mulally did just that. He cut operating costs in North America by $5 billion, laid off 10,000 salaried workers, sold off legendary brands such as Jaguar, Land Rover, Aston Martin, and Volvo, and borrowed $23 billion to keep the company afloat, even offering up the Ford "blue oval" brand as collateral.

All those moves would be tough enough for most CEOs, but Mulally took it a step further. While he was putting out short-term fires, he established a disciplined program to make sure the company would thrive in the years to come. As he explains: "The goal is always the same, no matter what. It's always long-term profitable growth. If you're not growing you're dying. You have to build products people want and value, plus you have to improve your productivity and quality every year. So it is all about the long term and how it puts everything in context for the short-term decisions—everything. We

Figure 1. Alan Mulally's "Working Together: Principles and Practices"

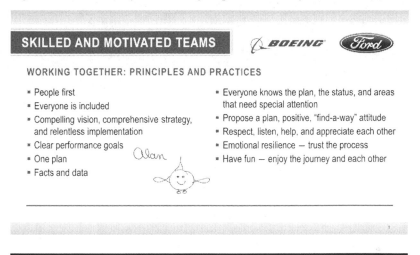

always, always look at the long term, which helps us do everything that's right for the short term."[17]

Mulally keeps his formula for long-term, profitable growth on a simple card titled "Working Together: Principles and Practices."[18]

He says this one piece of paper summarizes everything he learned, and used, at both Boeing, where he turned around the commercial airliner division, and Ford. He used this list of principles in every one of his legendary Business Plan Review strategy meetings, which he held every week for 45 years spanning his tenure at the two companies. "This is who I am and what I do," explains Mulally.

Everybody on a team is expected to follow every one of the "working together" principles and practices—all the time. In essence, Mulally uses his card to get his top executive team to focus on the company's long-term strategy, its implementation, and the team behavior needed to make it all happen. By constantly driving home the same set of principles and practices, he makes sure his lieutenants understand his plan and what it will take to execute it. "The biggest problem with communications is the illusion that it occurs," he quips.

Put People First (Really)

Most companies give lip service to putting people first, but many CEOs still like to rule on high. Information is power, and sometimes an organization's culture leads to fiefdoms where many top employees are kept in the dark about what's really going on. Typically these executives aren't treated with respect and don't understand the long-term strategy of the company or why it is so crucial to its success.

When Mulally first arrived at Ford in late 2006 he saw a dysfunctional culture. The organization had become very fragmented and regionalized. For example, according to the book *American Icon*, Ford's European engineers deliberately designed cars so they couldn't be sold in America without expensive changes to meet safety requirements, and some of the best new technology in the United States was kept from the team in Europe.[19]

Any CEO knows that cultural change is hard and takes a long time. But if he was to save Ford, Mulally realized that he needed to quickly build a cohesive top management team that worked well together. He turned to the first item on his card: "People first."

Mulally started by looking at the performance reviews of both top and up-and-coming executives. After talking with Bill Ford and others in the company about talent, he put together a core team of 16 executives and organized them in a matrix. He selected four business unit leaders, one each for Asia/Pacific, Europe, North America, and South America. Across those regions he spread a dozen different functions such as manufacturing, engineering, marketing, human resources, legal, procurement, and product development. He picked for his team the senior leaders who had won the strong support of many other Ford employees.

The new CEO wanted his team to look at the world the way it was—not the way they wanted it to be. In those days Ford was hierarchical, and people guarded information very carefully. Many of the top executives didn't even know about the impending $17 billion loss. Mulally had the finance people share all of Ford's financial and operational data, and for the first time the executive team saw how bad the situation was. He explained the severity of the overcapacity in Ford's factories, the lack of quality in the product line, and how they were losing money on every brand. This was a necessary and collective splash of cold water to the face.

In companies with strong cultures, bad news travels up. In weak cultures, employees are afraid to flag a faulty product or a delayed launch. Companies with that kind of culture can pay a high price. For example, the Silicon Valley "bad boy" behavior at Uber was left to fester. No one had the courage to call out the win-at-all-costs behavior of some top executives. This eventually helped lead to the ouster of CEO Travis Kalanick in mid-2017.[20]

Build Respect

Another key tenet on Mulally's card was the idea that "everyone needs to know the plan." So he shared with his team his core vision, which he built around Henry Ford's original idea of making the automobile available to the masses. While doing his research before coming to the company, he had come across an old advertisement Henry Ford had taken out in the *Saturday Evening Post* in 1925 of a couple and their Model T on a bluff overlooking the company's new River Rouge plant. The caption read: "Opening the highways to all mankind."[21] Mulally used that ad—a copy of which hung in his office—as inspiration to get his executive team to respect the Ford heritage, produce great products, create a strong business, and make a better world. "There will be people looking to make money in the short term but that's not the business that we were in at Ford. We were in the business of safe and efficient transportation for everyone around the world, and the only way to do that is to go long."

That new vision meant taking apart almost everything that had been built over the past decades. The team agreed to close factories, focus on the Ford brands, and divest Jaguar, Aston Martin, Land Rover, Volvo, and Mercury. They also committed to invest in a full product line of new cars, SUVs, and trucks, and to the idea that every new vehicle that Ford designed and made would try to be best in class in terms of quality, safety, connectivity, and environmental impact. "You can imagine what those conversations were like," recalls Mulally. "I was undoing much of what had been put in place, but I stressed that everything we do in the near term is going to have an eye toward building a profitable, growing company for the long term."

To make his vision a reality Mulally had to replace Ford's dysfunctional culture with one based on respect, honesty, and transparency—again, all principles pulled from his "Working Together" card. Not every top executive, as it turns out, was up to the task. "You have to be very clear about expected behaviors," says Mulally. "And once you agree on process and behaviors, the most important thing I did as a leader was to hold myself and my team accountable for following the process and the expected behaviors." For example, if someone was talking at a meeting when someone else was presenting, Mulally would simply stop the meeting and look at the individual until the talking stopped. One Ford executive on the team was in the habit of fiercely attacking any idea with which he disagreed. Mulally would ask him to apologize for acting that way, and he would—at every meeting, over and over again.

Finally, Mulally went to the executive's office with a simple message. "You know the plan here is not to behave so you have to apologize every week," he said.

"I don't know whether I can do that," the executive replied. "And besides, Ford promoted me over the years for behaving in just that way."

"It's okay," Mulally said. "I understand."

"It's okay?"

"It's okay," Mulally answered, "because it means you've decided that this is not the place for you, and you'd be better off moving on."

The executive did, in the end, move on. In the years since, Mulally says he rarely had to fire someone, because if you clarify the rules up front and hold yourself and everyone else accountable, those who can't evolve are likely to realize it—and leave.

Be Brutally Honest

Mulally also worked hard on transparency. At the weekly business review meetings, he had his executives stick color-coded charts related to important projects on a white board. A green chart indicated the project was going well, a yellow one signaled a few things needed tweaking, and a red one meant the project was in trouble. "We needed to get the yellows and reds described so we could all work together to turn the yellows and reds to greens," he recalls.

At one early meeting, Mulally looked up at the white board and saw all green charts. So he said: "We're losing $17 billion. Is there anything that's not going well?" All the executives were staring at the floor. They were afraid to report any problems because, in the old days, whenever someone raised an issue, they seemed to disappear—permanently.

At the next business review meeting, Mark Fields, who was running the company's North American operations, had the courage to put up a red chart. The new Ford Edge crossover was suffering some suspension problems, and the launch of this crucial new model would have to be delayed—potentially costing the company millions it could ill afford to lose at the time. As Mulally recalls: "He looked at me, and I looked at him, and I clapped. Some in the room must have thought it was the signal for the two large doors behind me to open up and for two security guards to remove Mark. It didn't happen. Instead I asked, 'What can we do to help?'" A few team members had some suggestions, and a couple of weeks later Fields got the parts he needed from other Ford divisions around the world. Before long his red chart had turned to green.

The following week the charts looked like a rainbow—a lot of red and yellow and a smattering of green. And right there Mulally knew that his team was starting to work together and that as a result they would be able to solve problems no matter what challenges they encountered—whether the financial crisis, safety issues, or new competitors. He now had a process in place that was reliable, and a team that was following it every week, every quarter, and every year.

Achieve Profitable Growth for All

Any CEO who wants to achieve long-term, profitable growth must have a clear way to measure progress. Otherwise it's easy to let a company's long-term vision fall to the wayside, as pressing daily issues take everyone's time and attention. In Mulally's case, he used something he called "profitable growth for all," or PGA.

Yes, Mulally had gotten his team to start pulling together, which helped put out fires like the delayed launch of the Ford Edge. But he also felt it was crucial to get his executive team focused on the company's long-term future. One key to achieving a long-term focus is to make sure, as his card puts it, that the team has "clear goals." That's where PGA comes in.

The beauty of PGA, Mulally says, is that it gets everyone absolutely focused on the long-term fundamentals. Simply put, PGA is revenue times margins (profits). The goal is to use those measures to achieve a 10% to 15% compounded annual growth rate. Why 10% to 15%? He explains that if the profits aren't going up 10% to 15% a year, "you're not going to have a viable business."

So how do you achieve that, especially at a company like Ford, which was slated to lose $17 billion in a single year? The only way to raise revenue is to make products and provide services people want and value, and good companies improve their margins every year by improving quality and productivity. Mulally says the trick is to work both of those levers.

This is how the math works: If you increase both revenue and margins by roughly 5% to 7% a year, you get that 10% to 15% profit growth. The "all" in PGA refers to *all* the company's stakeholders—consumers, employees, suppliers, investors, and communities. "Everyone is going to benefit," he says. "We are creating profitable growth and value for all."

During each of Mulally's business review meetings, he asked his 16 top executives to apply PGA to a five-year horizon; imagine five bars representing profits going out five years, and each one going up 15%. That simple exercise got the executives to look five years out every week, every quarter, every year—even while they were dealing with short-term crises. Explains Mulally: "The expectation is that you'll make the commitment this year for profit, and once you do that you're going to have to put another bar out there five years out that's high enough so that when you discount it back, you're going to get your 15% in profit growth. So the 15% is not just the profits going up but also the value of your company going up. Isn't that cool?"

By sharing his formula, Mulally got everyone in the company working on revenue *and* everyone working on the margins. In other words, everyone in the entire corporation was focused on the same goal. Mulally says it unleashed creativity throughout the organization. It gave directors confidence that the business was moving in the right direction. Even the Wall Street analysts knew what to look for on every earnings call, and looked to see how the company was doing against its 15% profit goal.

Profit goals aren't the only thing you need, however. You need measurements for every one of your stakeholders, and they should all be moving in a positive direction. You need to know how your employees, customers, bankers, and suppliers feel. Are you creating value for all of them?

Mulally and his team looked at a variety of metrics every quarter and forecast them out five years, always adjusting depending on the facts on the ground. For example, when Ford decided to move toward electrified vehicles or switch its F-150 pickup to an aluminum body, the executive team always asked what such a move would mean to every one of those constituencies. "By looking at those metrics regularly and letting the data shape our detailed plans, we got pretty good at making decisions," says Mulally.

Of course, it's not easy to make projections five years out. Mulally recalls how his executive team struggled with Ford's employee satisfaction data. In the early days, when the company was bleeding, the numbers didn't look good. Employee engagement was only at 24%. Mulally's team needed to come to an agreement on what the five-year target should be on employee engagement. What should the slope be to get to where they wanted to be five years out? The team didn't know how to make such a vague projection.

The CEO told them to just make it a positive slope, and they could always modify as they made progress on the plan. "That was a breakthrough for everyone," he says. "The key was everyone got feedback on employee satisfaction in the Business Plan Review meetings over and over again." Over time, the team realized that it was important for all of Ford's employees to feel like their jobs had meaning, that they were able to contribute to Ford's turnaround, that they were part of something bigger than themselves, and that it was the job of top management to communicate that.

By the time Mulally left Ford in 2014, employee satisfaction had hit 89%—one of the highest rates in all of corporate America.

Executive Summary
Creating a Culture for Going Long

1. One of the toughest challenges any CEO faces is staying focused on a long-term strategy while having to deal with short-term distractions. Contentious earnings calls, a division whose sales are slipping, a product launch that's fallen behind, or a key manager who's demoralizing the troops—all these short-term crises can distract the best of CEOs and their team from driving home a long-term strategy.

2. When going long, the goal is to create a culture that is always focused on long-term, profitable growth. You need to develop a team that's open enough and trusting enough to do what it takes to build products people want and improve your productivity every year.

3. Create a culture that's brutally honest about what's working and not working within the organization. Companies that let problems fester end up paying the price in the long term.

4. It is important for a company's rank and file to feel like their jobs have meaning, that they are able to contribute to the company's success, and that they are part of something bigger than themselves. It is the job of top management to communicate that.

Advice from Alan Mulally to Other CEOs

At Boeing and Ford, we knew it was all about skilled and motivated people "working together" to deliver an exciting, sustainable, profitably growing company for the benefit of all the stakeholders. The "working together" management system is a business process as well as an expected way of behaving for all the participants.

The unique contribution of the leader and the leadership team is to hold themselves responsible and accountable for implementing the "working together" business system—both the reliable business process and the expected behavior of all the participants. "Working together" allows a smart and healthy team to deliver products and services people want and value, with everyone improving quality and productivity and with everyone feeling the true satisfaction and joy of meaningful accomplishment.

Leadership service is such an honor. To serve is to live!

Chapter 2

CVS Takes a $2 Billion Hit— on Purpose

By banning cigarette sales, CVS Health's Larry Merlo took a huge short-term risk to make credible his long-term quest to turn his pharmacy company into a healthcare giant.

> *The opportunity to link your brand's purpose to your actions is tangible, and should never be underestimated in terms of the amount of impact it has internally and externally.*
> —Larry Merlo, president and CEO of CVS Health

Sometimes executing a promising long-term strategy means taking a heavy hit in short-term profits. That's exactly the situation CEO Larry Merlo found himself facing in 2014, when he decided to become the first major pharmacy retailer to stop selling cigarettes—a decision that cost the business $2 billion a year in revenues and a 7% drop in its stock price the day he announced the plan.

Merlo, however, deeply believed that pulling tobacco products from his shelves was the right thing to do. He saw that the markets were shifting and he needed new sources of long-term growth. The future of this $178 billion-a-year company rested in becoming a leading provider of health services, and it was hypocritical, he believed, for a company that was trying to make its customers healthier to also sell them cigarettes.

He is one of a small group of powerful CEOs who have sacrificed short-term performance for the sake of a long-term strategy. Such behavior is fairly common today with fast-growing high-tech companies. Netflix sacrificed its mail-order DVD business to build itself into a streaming video giant. Tesla's Elon Musk has taken years of short-term losses in pursuit of building a global electric car company. (Whether he will succeed in this endeavor remains to be seen.) Amazon's Jeff Bezos took losses for years and used his cash to grab market share for his e-tailer. Today Amazon is the leading player in that space.

While it's not unexpected for relatively new companies like Netflix, Tesla, and Amazon to forgo profits to grow, it is much more unusual for big, long-established companies like CVS Health to take a short-term hit. After all, investors value such companies for their ability to grow sales and earn steadily year after year. Any variation from that pattern is bound to raise alarm bells. For a CEO, then, it takes real courage to make a move that so defies the expectations and comfort zones of investors. There have been a few other cases in business history. In the late 1990s, for example, the investment firm Charles Schwab saw that internet trading would hit it like a tsunami. CEO and founder Charles Schwab decided he had to reinvent his cost structure by going digital. Over a six-month period the company suffered a 22% loss in revenues and a 25% drop in its share price while it retooled and cut its trading costs by 70%. A year later Schwab had picked up a million new customers.[22]

When CVS's Merlo decided to jettison $2 billion in annual cigarette sales, it was anything but an easy decision. Wall Street would not be happy with the pharmacy giant taking a $2 billion haircut. Merlo, however, thought the gamble worth it—he believed that in the long haul he could get much faster growth from health services than his retail business.

To take advantage of this trend, however, he had to transform CVS into a healthcare company. In 2007 CVS acquired Caremark, America's leading pharmacy-benefits management company. Caremark processes prescriptions for clients that pay for drugs, usually large employers and health plans, and uses its size and buying clout to negotiate with drug makers and pharmacies for the best deals. Caremark helps businesses keep their employees' health costs down, and the more it could do that, the more corporate clients would use its services. After all, a lot of money is at stake. Studies show that 50% of all Americans suffer from some sort of chronic disease,[23] and people not taking their medication raises healthcare costs in the United States by as much as $300 billion a year.[24] For example, a person with diabetes who fails to stick to an insulin regime is apt to fall ill, and it could then cost six to eight times as much to treat the person, sending insurance premiums soaring. "We have a lot of clients," says Merlo, "counting on us to help keep their employees healthy."[25]

At the same time, CVS began opening walk-in retail mini-clinics in its stores called MinuteClinic, where nurse practitioners treat individuals for common illnesses, check blood pressure, take cholesterol readings, offer advice on diet and exercise, and, yes, help people quit smoking. As of 2017 CVS had more than 1,100 of these retail clinics, which have provided a steady source of growth and profits.

In the years leading up to the removal of tobacco products—as CVS became more of a healthcare company and less of a convenience store—it started to get pushback from hospitals, corporate benefit managers, and other customers. "Our clients started raising the question, 'How can you be a healthcare company and sell tobacco?'" A similar debate arose among the top executive team at CVS. The company's chief medical officer would raise the issue of tobacco and its ill effects on health, or management would hear complaints about selling cigarettes from some of the nurse practitioners working in its MinuteClinic.

Seek Grassroots Buy-In

One thing that's crucial when making a strategic decision that will be costly in the short term is getting buy-in throughout the organization. CEOs who decide it is necessary to take a financial hit to achieve a long-term goal must get the support not only of investors (for more on this topic, see chapter 4) but also of the executive team and the rank and file. Not doing so can endanger the entire long-term strategy. If the company's employees don't feel that the CEO is truly serious about change, then executing that change will be a monumental challenge.

Merlo, a pharmacist by education, had the right background to get buy-in for his strategy. He joined CVS Pharmacy in 1990 and rose through the ranks by completing a string of successful retail pharmacy acquisitions before becoming president and CEO in 2011. Throughout 2013 he met two or three times every month with his top executives and debated the tobacco issue. Was CVS a convenience store that had a pharmacy in the back, or a pharmacy that offered convenience goods? The team decided that CVS was the latter, and that conviction made it easier to justify dropping tobacco sales. And besides, the potential benefits were great. Healthcare providers would see CVS's move as a positive and therefore would be more likely to do business with the company. Also, it would be easier to recruit and retain health-conscious and purpose-seeking millennials to work at the company.

Over time, Merlo and his team developed a clear and coherent argument for the move to drop tobacco and worked hard to show how it would fit into the long-term vision of the company. Because the company's two-paragraph vision statement at the time was vague and confusing, Merlo formed a small task force of managers and asked them to come up with a statement that not only was simpler but also truly captured the new long-term vision he had for the company. The team delivered a concise and memorable line: "To help people on their path to better health." Says the CEO: "That line brought to light our purpose to others in the organization and it made it clear that by dropping tobacco we're walking the walk." Indeed, when he told the company's head of tobacco sales that he was thinking of dropping the product, the manager said: "I'm the last person in the world you have to worry about. It's the right thing to do."

Get the Board on Board

Now Merlo had to sell the idea to his board. Any CEO who wants to take a significant near-term hit for the sake of a long-term strategy of course has to win the backing of the directors. The best approach is for CEOs to make sure they build a board populated with directors who have a long-term mindset before the need arises to take a financial hit. CEOs should look for directors who are involved enough in the business so that they have a firm grasp of the long-term strategy and what sacrifices will be necessary in the short run to make it a reality. Without support from the board, the chances of a CEO's long-term strategy succeeding are slight.

To lay the groundwork for his new strategy, Merlo discussed his concept with a few key CVS directors before presenting it to the entire board. That meant most of the board members would already be aware of the initiative by the time he unveiled the full plan. At a board meeting in January 2014, Merlo explained to his directors the contradiction of going into healthcare while at the same time selling tobacco. He outlined the $2 billion in lost annual sales—$1.5 billion from tobacco, along with $500 million from gum, candy, and other items bought by cigarette purchasers—but argued that tobacco was a headwind that would prevent the company from pursuing new growth opportunities in healthcare. In addition, selling tobacco put the CVS brand in a negative light. As part of his proposal to the board Merlo suggested changing the name of the company from CVS Caremark to CVS Health. The one big bet Merlo was making was that he would lose people who were using CVS as a convenience store but would keep those using it as a pharmacy—the very customers he wanted to court because that end of the business enjoyed higher margins than retail.

What ultimately helped him win his argument at that meeting was that, over the years, Merlo and his CEO predecessors had assembled a very forward-looking board—directors who understood the value of managing a company for the long haul. For example, David

Dorman, the chairman of the CVS board at the time, is the founding partner of Centerview Capital Technology, a successful private equity firm known for its patient investment style.

Even so, Merlo says he was a "nervous wreck" at the meeting. In the end, however, he ended up walking away with a lot of confidence, because he felt he had 100% support from the board. One director, Tony White, told Merlo "not to be shy about telling the tobacco story to the world." It was counsel that came in handy when the going got rough. In February 2014 Merlo announced that by October 1 of that year, CVS would remove tobacco from all of its then 7,600 pharmacies. A few days later, the CEO had a fourth-quarter earnings call, and CVS's stock took a 7% hit. Merlo said he deliberately announced the bad news during a quarter where he could also announce strong financial results. Otherwise the damage to the company's stock market capitalization might have been even greater.

Keep All Stakeholders in the Loop

When short-term pressures from Wall Street mount, it helps for CEOs to keep all stakeholders focused on the benefits of the long-term strategy. Support from the board, as we've seen, is crucial, but it also pays to let employees, customers, and clients know that you're about to embark on a radically different strategy. And that's what Merlo did in the ensuing months.

He stressed both to Wall Street and to his employees how dropping tobacco opened doors for new partnerships and affiliations. Today, the company has partnerships with 70 health systems across the country, where CVS MinuteClinic will refer customers to certain doctors or hospitals, and vice versa. "I'm not sure we would have been able to have formed so many partnerships if we had still been selling cigarettes, given the health-conscious nature of those institutions," argues Merlo. While it's hard to say that CVS won a particular affiliation strictly from the tobacco decision, it certainly helped give it an edge by showing the world that the company was serious about healthcare.

Merlo also launched an internal communication initiative and a social media campaign, and gave extensive interviews to major publications such as the *Wall Street Journal,* the *New York Times,* and *USA Today.* He explained the meaning of the company's new name—CVS Health—and reinforced the idea that it was all about helping people become healthier. Merlo says he was amazed at how every time he brought up banning cigarettes, almost everyone he spoke to had a story about how tobacco impacted them or someone they knew. CVS Health received cards and letters and online postings from all over the country, not only from employees and customers but also from celebrities, sports figures, and even politicians. First Lady Michelle Obama gave the company a "thumbs-up" for the move.[26] Anti-smoking groups also chimed in with rare praise for corporate America: "CVS' announcement to stop selling tobacco products . . . sends a resounding message to the entire retail industry and to its customers that pharmacies should not be in the business of selling tobacco," said Matthew Myers, president of the Washington-based Campaign for Tobacco-Free Kids. "This is truly an example of a corporation leading and setting a new standard."[27]

The move gave the company a different face to present to the community. "It created a sense of pride," says Merlo. "I think every employee felt they were part of the decision to drop tobacco because of the role they were playing in helping people get healthier." Around the same time, CVS Health launched a program to help people quit smoking. One pharmacist shared how two of his customers were an older couple who smoked. They told the pharmacist that they would quit when CVS did, and they did.

Throughout those tough months after the tobacco decision, Merlo also sent a clear and consistent message to Wall Street analysts. On quarterly calls that year, he told them what the headwinds would be and what the benefits would be. He shared with analysts what he thought were opportunities for growth and how tobacco was a barrier to this. He explained how the move was not linear, that CVS Health was not going to lose a dollar here on tobacco and make it up somewhere else on the same day but that he was confident that in the long run they would make that up from healthcare. Some analysts expressed reservations, but by clearly and consistently explaining his long-term strategy, Merlo eventually won over most of his investors.

Execute, Execute, Execute

After CEOs have achieved buy-in for their long-term strategies from all the key constituencies, they need to develop a leadership plan for execution. This requires a lot of heavy lifting. One key point is not to get distracted by the fact that your competitors might not follow suit—it can be lonely out there when pursuing a radically new direction.

When Merlo set out to execute his tobacco plan, his team had to make sure that cigarettes were removed from all 7,600 stores by its self-imposed deadline of October 1, 2014. If the team was 99% successful that would mean 76 CVS stores would still be selling cigarettes after the deadline, and all it would take to blow the credibility of the project was for one enterprising reporter to find a pack of Marlboros or Kents still on sale behind the counter. That never happened. Another factor that made executing the plan difficult was that CVS's competitors didn't follow suit. Walgreen's, Rite Aid, and other competitors argued that they want to help people quit smoking but don't want to tell them what to buy and what not to buy. They don't want to be seen as part of the "nanny state," a stance that made them popular among certain segments of the buying public.

Even so, as the CVS tobacco story became more widely known and understood, the pressure from Wall Street subsided and the benefits of the long-term tobacco-free strategy began to take hold. A study in the American Journal of Public Health revealed that in the markets where CVS stopped selling tobacco, some 95 million fewer packs of cigarettes were sold over the first eight months.[28] That is impressive; still, it represented just a 1% reduction in tobacco sales. Ellen Hahn of the Tobacco Policy Research Program at the University of Kentucky explained that one chain not selling tobacco can have only a limited effect, and other methods such as public smoking bans and higher taxes on cigarettes are more effective. Even so, she argues that "every little bit helps, because they are such a large chain. If every pharmacy would follow suit, that would be best. But this sends a clear message that pharmacies should not be selling tobacco."[29]

Simultaneously, CVS's new pharmacy benefits management services and retail clinics business took off. The pharmacy benefits service (which does not include retail pharmacy) grew its revenues from $88 million in 2014 to $120 million in 2016. Over the same period, the retail pharmacy and retail clinics businesses grew from $66 million in annual revenues to $81 million. And both segments are profitable today. At the time of the tobacco announcement in February 2014, CVS stock was trading at $73 a share. A year later, despite that initial 7% dip, it was trading at $100, although as of the writing of this book some of those gains have been given back as pharmacy margins have come under increased pressure.

Merlo continued his long-term quest to position CVS Health as a healthcare leader, and in 2017 he announced that his company would acquire Aetna, one of America's biggest health insurance companies, for $69 billion. Routine healthcare is shifting from the doctor's office to online apps, over-the-phone services, and retail clinics like the ones CVS Health operates. Merlo's idea is that the best way to make consumers healthier is to make the experience as seamless as possible.[30]

Around the same time, to attack obesity, one of America's biggest health problems, CVS removed trans fats from its store-brand foods and began working with suppliers to sell healthier alternates. It has moved healthier foods to the front of its stores, reserving roughly a quarter of front checkout space to what it calls "better for you" snacks. The company also began labeling shelves as "heart healthy" and "gluten free."

The move will certainly result in lower sales of candy bars and cheese puffs, but in the long run Merlo believes it is the right thing to do both for his customers and employees and for the bottom line.

Executive Summary
Going Long Sometimes Requires Taking a Short-Term Hit

1. By banning cigarette sales, CVS Health CEO Larry Merlo took a huge risk that hurt the company's earnings and stock. He realized, however, that to become a credible healthcare brand, CVS Health could not be seen peddling products that can cause disease and death.
2. It's essential when making a strategic decision that will be costly in the short term to get grassroots buy-in throughout the organization. If the company's employees don't feel that the CEO is truly serious about change, then executing that change will be a monumental challenge.
3. Any CEO who wants to take a significant near-term hit for the sake of a long-term strategy has to win the backing of the board. The best approach is for CEOs to make sure they build a board populated with directors who have a long-term mindset before they need to take a financial hit.
4. After CEOs have achieved buy-in for their long-term strategies from all the key constituencies, they will need to develop a leadership plan for execution. One key point is not to get distracted by the fact that your competitors might not follow suit—it can be lonely out there when pursuing a radically new direction.

Advice from Larry Merlo to Other CEOs

The opportunity to link your brand to your purpose is tangible. You can never underestimate the amount of impact it has internally and externally on our colleagues, customers, and new customers. When you adopt a new purpose and make a dramatic strategy change you have to tell the story—and not be shy about telling the story.

You have to articulate the reason for the change to your board, your management team, your employees, and the community. I constantly explained how our purpose links to how we define opportunities for growth. After we announced that we were tobacco-free, we engaged in an ambitious communication campaign both through the press and social media. We launched a program to help people quit smoking. As our story began to be told by others, it helped validate what we were doing.

Linking our new strategy to our purpose of helping people on their path to better health gave me confidence. It made our clients in healthcare feel more comfortable working with us. It also has helped us attract the best and brightest people. You see it in the questions the millennials ask today: "What's the purpose of the company and how does that purpose come to life in my job?"

In the end, I think banning cigarette sales serves as a constant reminder for us of that balance between short-term actions and long-term thinking.

Chapter 3

Lead with a Purpose and the Profits Will Follow

When it comes to managing for the long run, Unilever CEO Paul Polman believes that focusing on the multi-stakeholder is a better business model than shareholder primacy.

> *Our system is there to satisfy a few billion people in the world. Not a few billionaires.*
>
> —Paul Polman, CEO of Unilever

When Paul Polman became CEO of Unilever in September 2009, the financial crisis was in full swing. Lehman Brothers had collapsed a year earlier, the stock market was in a free fall, and consumer demand was drying up. Polman had been hired away from Nestle to right the listing consumer products giant, the first outside CEO in the company's 100+ year history. The Anglo-Dutch company sells more than 400 brands to some 2.5 billion customers in 190 countries, including Dove, Lifebuoy, Hellman's mayonnaise, Lipton, and Ben & Jerry's ice cream. The previous CEO had streamlined the company by selling businesses and closing factories, but growth had stalled.

Before assuming his new position, Polman spent several months studying the situation and decided that what Unilever needed was a commitment to the longer term. As he explains: "The measures Unilever had been taking were increasingly short term, making the company's situation worse. One of the things that Unilever was known for was juggling advertising and promotion costs or selling off brands to make the last quarter's profit commitment. That's not a good strategy if you're in packaged goods and you want to grow your business."[31] The company was also heavily underinvesting, allocating only 2% of revenues on capital spending.

On the first day of his new job Polman shocked investors—and his board—by announcing that Unilever would no longer give earnings guidance. He followed up by ditching quarterly profit reporting. He saw the move as a way to send a clear signal that he planned to run the business for the long term—plus, he says he figured that he was not going to get fired on the first day in the office. "I wanted no more calls with analysts explaining our quarterly profit and earnings per share delivery. There will always be short-term fluctuations on those metrics based on the weather or the timing of Ramadan or such like but discussing these only exacerbates the short-term management of profits."

Investors—who thought the move meant that more bad news must be coming—headed for the exits, and Unilever's shares dropped 6% over that month. Undaunted, Polman set out to re-create Unilever into a company that put employees, customers, and communities first. This approach, he believed, would be the best way to take care of shareholders in the long run.

It worked. In 2017 sales hit $58 billion, up 3% from the previous year. As of the writing of this book, Unilever has enjoyed 37 quarters of dividend growth and a total shareholder return of 285% since 2008; that's better than the market indexes and best in its industry.

Create a Purpose beyond Profits

In this age of rampant short-termism, CEOs like Polman are rare. Most succumb to constant pressure to deliver quarterly results, often at the expense of the future prosperity of their company. CEOs who best manage for the long term have to cater to their shareholders but also do much more than that. Managing for the long term means creating a business model that takes other constituencies into account.

It means running a business profitably but also making sure employees, customers, suppliers, and the community at large benefit from the activities of a corporation.

We're not talking here about setting up a Corporate Social Responsibility department or launching a feel-good marketing campaign. In the best long-term business models, the concerns and needs of all constituencies become a core part of the way a company conducts its business. Google, for example, tries, among other things, to be a good steward of the environment—it now gets 100% of its energy from renewable sources.[32] Healthcare giant Kaiser Permanente says it exists "to provide high-quality, affordable health care services and to improve the health of our members and the communities we serve."[33] That strong focus on the people it serves has helped Kaiser consistently rank at the top of surveys measuring quality healthcare.[34] Twitter's mission statement is "to give everyone the power to create and share ideas and information instantly, without barriers,"[35] and the social media platform has become instrumental in fomenting political change (think the Arab Spring and Donald Trump), for better or for worse.

The point is that all effective long-term visions include a purpose far beyond maximizing shareholder return. Focusing on a broader target can energize employees, help shape short-term decisions, and boost the bottom line. Perhaps the starkest example of a socially focused long-term strategy is Unilever, whose mission statement reads simply: "To add vitality to life. We meet everyday needs for nutrition, hygiene and personal care with brands that help people feel good, look good and get more out of life."[36] As Polman puts it, "We make it very clear to our employees that our objective is to serve the world's consumers and to serve the world's issues and only by doing this will our shareholders be long-term successful."

After Polman jettisoned quarterly earnings reports, he set about to create a viable business model that would ensure a long, prosperous future for Unilever. In a 2010 call to arms he dubbed the Unilever Sustainable Living Plan (USLP), Polman defined his long-term strategy. The company promised to cut its environmental footprint by half and, at the same time, double revenues. The company also promised to increase its social impact by improving the well-being of one billion people by, for example, persuading them to wash their hands or brush their teeth, or by selling them foods with less salt or fat. "The most important thing we did," says Polman, "was to create a biz model that was captured in the USLP."

Getting there, however, was not an easy journey. Polman faced skeptical employees, directors, and investors and some years later a $143 billion hostile takeover bid by the Brazilian private equity firm 3G, which owns a large share of Kraft Heinz (which he repelled).[37] Here's how he applied long-term thinking to overcome those obstacles and give Unilever a clear shot at a bright future.

The Purpose and Plan Must Align

Polman's plan to make society's challenges the focus of Unilever's business would require a mental shift, a refocusing from the executive suite down through middle management to the truck drivers who deliver its products to the 76,000 suppliers that provide Unilever's raw materials. The CEO also realized that any long-term strategy he devised had to resonate with everyone in the organization. What he did calls to mind Jim Collins, author of the best-selling book *Built to Last*, and his observation that "companies that enjoy enduring success must have a core purpose and core values that remain fixed while their strategies and practices endlessly adapt to a changing world."[38]

The core Polman nurtured was Unilever's long history of mixing business with altruism. The new CEO had spent time studying the company's history and found there the values that would drive his strategy. He learned that William Lever founded the company to better the lives of his workers and of society in general. Lever had talked about shared prosperity well before anyone else. He called his hand soap Lifebuoy because he thought it would help improve people's lives by making hygiene commonplace (Victorian Britain was not known for its cleanliness). The man brought purpose to everything he did. He guaranteed wages to workers who went off to World War I.

He introduced pensions to the UK. He took his wife's name—Leverhulme—when he was elected to the House of Lords in 1906, a symbolic act to show his support for women's rights.

"So what I thought was, why not go back to this?" recalls Polman. "Coming out of financial crisis and as a new CEO, I didn't want to just say run faster, run harder. That wasn't a very motivating strategy." He looked at some megatrends emerging or worsening—climate change, wealth inequality, hunger, poverty, and disease—and asked whether Unilever could become a net contributor to society rather than a taker. "It would be the best guarantee," says Polman, "that what we were doing we would be embraced by society."

To sell his strategy, he held his first executive board meeting at Port Sunlight, a housing complex near Liverpool, England, that the Lord Lever built for his 3,500 soap factory workers in the late nineteenth and early twentieth centuries. This model village, named after the company's first household soap, Sunlight, is made up of 800 well-constructed Tudor-style houses, the Lady Lever Art Gallery, a cottage hospital, schools, a concert hall, an open-air swimming pool, a church, and a temperance hotel.[39]

The message sent to Unilever's board and to directors was clear. Polman was going to secure the future of the company by reaching back into its past. He explained how the company planned to decouple its growth from its environmental impact, and how it would maximize its social impact by improving the health and well-being of one billion people. "We were excited but scared stiff," says Polman. "No one else had gone this direction, as it required transformative partnerships beyond Unilever alone. The board was especially nervous because we put 50 targets out there. A lot of people said I wasn't going to last, and that I wasn't going to be there in 10 years to see this through."

Embed Purpose throughout the Organization

Any CEO wanting to create a purpose-led organization must find ways to win over both internal and external constituencies. This requires a lot more than simply making pronouncements about having a "purpose." It means making sure your employees and suppliers not only understand the raison d'être of the company but also act in ways that support that purpose. The purpose must be part of the organization's DNA, with hardheaded metrics tracked to measure progress.

In Polman's case, he invited a broad constituency of people to be part of that journey and help integrate USLP into the way the company did business. That meant taking a total value-chain approach. Says Polman: "You might outsource your supply chain but you can't outsource your responsibility."

He asked his team to look at packaging waste, water usage, and labor standards across the whole supply chain, from farm to factory. He also disbanded Unilever's Corporate Social Responsibility department, with the specific intent of sending a message that the company's extensive social commitments needed to be integrated into the business targets for every brand and in every market, with no exceptions.

Whenever he got pushback from his executives he would explain one of the main driving forces behind his decision—the fact that millennials, who made up half of Unilever's workforce, were asking for more responsible and purpose-driven business models. The enormous economic opportunity was equally becoming more apparent. More and more consumers were looking for responsible products and companies. He told his team to think about it in terms of a dinner table conservation. As he explains: "When you go to someone's house and you start talking about where you work and what you do, and they start to be critical about your company, you won't be happy." Polman wanted everyone to be able to be proud of working for the company. He wanted them to feel energized.

As expected, of course, the change took its toll. In the first few years Polman ended up rotating or letting go 50% of his top 100 people. Some executives simply weren't good fits in a strategic sense— if Polman wanted to grow the company he'd need more marketing and fewer finance people. But many simply were not behind his vision, and these individuals were asked to move on.

Perhaps the greatest challenge, however, was for Polman and his team to figure out how to ensure that what they were doing was really driving their results. "The danger," says Polman, "was that we'd get carried away and try to help everyone who's out there." To make sure employees understood the link between his sustainability plan and what drove the business, Polman gave his team lots of training on how to measure progress and how to handle trade-offs. The executive team, for example, spent a lot of time on measuring and sequencing, on seeing what was possible and what was not, and on naming priorities while letting go of other things, all the while communicating those findings down the ranks.

First, they measured the impact of Unilever's products across the value chain. For example, for a product like Dove soap, they asked questions such as: What's the total carbon emissions of a shower, including the manufacture of the soap and the heating of the water? What kind of packaging is being used? They then came up with a total footprint of the product. Once the footprint was established, they could focus on the environmental impact of each brand and seek out ways to lower it.

Next, they figured out each brand's social purpose. "Our most powerful brands," says Polman, "were those that were addressing issues. With Dove, we created a campaign about self-esteem for young girls. Lifebuoy was about helping a young child in the developing world have a better chance of reaching the age of five through better hygiene."

Persuade Wall Street That Sustainability Pays

Polman says it took six years of hard work before the sustainable living plan was really embedded in the culture. Along the way he was (and still is) the target of Wall Street skeptics who often questioned whether Polman's sustainability program was worth it. Polman told them that the USLP continued to boost sales in a tough global market, helped the company attract employees, reduced costs and risk, and was a key driver of the company's reputation. He argued that the company's global hand-washing campaign, which is backed by the United Nations and health ministers in Africa and Asia, lifted sales of Lifebuoy soap. Dove's self-esteem marketing campaign for young women, meanwhile, helped the soap become the company's best-selling brand in the United States. Eliminating all waste to landfills for all its factories and moving to green energy is saving over $600 million per year. Finally, the company's sense of purpose also helps attract and retain the best people. According to *Fortune* magazine, Unilever is one of the five most-searched-for employers on LinkedIn, behind Google, Apple, Microsoft, and Facebook.[40]

At the same time, Polman worked hard to cultivate the right kind of shareholders—those with a long-term horizon. He says a lot more investors would be interested in sustainability strategies if companies could give them some hard metrics that show progress and paybacks. After he stopped giving quarterly results, he went on investor road trips twice a year, stressing the company's long-term strategic story. He shared with them the company's plan for carbon and water reduction, innovations in packing material, and improvements in food nutrition and tied those metrics to the bottom line. The hard-number approach helped attract more long-term investors. "Your conversations become different both internally and externally," he says. It seemed to have worked: 70% of Unilever shareholders have held shares for more than seven years.

Battle Short-Termism

The bad news is that Polman believes the rest of the world—including the investment community—still has a long way to go when it comes to understanding the benefits of a long-term strategy. He believes short-termism is pervasive and rising. Part of that pressure, he argues, stems from the $12 or $13 *trillion* investments that in

2017 were earning zero or negative real interest rates. Global financial assets far exceed what the global economy needs. All this money
is chasing returns, and a large chunk of it is influenced by a handful
of mainly activist investors looking to make a short-term killing.
"Before you know it," says Polman, "you have 20% to 30% of your
shares owned by hedge funds that move in within a nanosecond and
start telling a CEO what to do."

Case in point: The Brazilian private equity firm 3G, which owns
a large stake of Kraft Heinz, targeted Unilever in February 2017. Kraft
Heinz made a takeover play at a 20% premium to Unilever's stock.
Polman was shocked and upset. His stock had been doing well over
the long haul—more than doubling over his tenure, which was a better
return than the overall market—and his investors seemed happy.
He had been cutting $1 billion a year at the company, but reinvesting
three-quarters of it back into the company for growth.

The problem was that Unilever's stock had stumbled in the previous year, slipping by more than 2% while the S&P 500 has soared
25%. Revenue growth had also slowed down. There were a number
of reasons for that—unfavorable foreign exchange rates following
Brexit and a slowing global economy, among others. But some investors were growing impatient, if not skeptical. As Jefferies sell-side
analyst Martin Deboo put it at the time: "A minority of investors I
speak to don't give two hoots about Unilever's Sustainable Living
Plan."[41] Polman responds by saying that many more investors voiced
their strong support for Unilever's long-term compounded growth
model.

Kraft Heinz saw an opportunity to create a global consumer
giant. Polman saw a company notorious for cost cutting that had in
recent years shed thousands of workers. "I couldn't think of two more
opposite philosophies coming together here," says Polman. "Frankly
someone who thinks they can buy us because they have a lot of money
and think they can leverage up our company and then run it with
an entirely different model that we don't think would lead to long-
term success—yeah, indeed that doesn't make much sense to me.

Our system is there to satisfy a few billion people in the world. Not a few billionaires."

Polman quickly went on the offensive, reaching out to investors and the press. He stressed his long-term investment record and how he was investing in products for the future. He also attacked 3G's slash-and-burn philosophy, arguing that it so far had not led to robust growth or strong financial returns for Kraft Heinz. The company withdrew its bid.

"Our board said our long-term compounded growth model is where the priority is," says Polman. "To do financial manipulations to give a few people some quick money is not something I would personally want to participate in. As long as I'm CEO I will fight that because it undermines the fundamental fabric of society or what we're trying to achieve. We have a responsibility as CEOs to have a model that works for all our stakeholders."

Executive Summary
Creating a Purpose-Driven Organization

1. Managing for the long term means creating a business model that takes other constituencies into account.
2. A company must have a purpose or core ideology, and a leader has to nurture the core before you can stimulate progress. Focusing on a broader target can energize employees, help shape short-term decisions, and boost the bottom line.
3. Any CEO wanting to create a purpose-led organization must find ways to win over both internal and external constituencies. It means making sure your employees and suppliers not only understand the raison d'être of the company but also act in ways that support that purpose.
4. Any CEO who wants to avoid becoming a target must think like an activist and cut costs or sell off businesses before the activists do it for them. The difference is when CEOs retain control of their destinies, they can achieve the same goals in ways that don't harm the long-term prospects of the company.

Advice from Paul Polman to Other CEOs

First of all, educate yourself on why managing for the long term is better by focusing on the multi-stakeholder, which is a better business model than shareholder primacy. Second, give your business a purpose. If CEOs can find a business model that deals with some of the world's challenges such as climate change, health, hunger, or human rights, it's far more motivational for their employees—plus it's an enormous business opportunity that they can seize. I'd also tell CEOs to actively engage with their shareholders and explain why their long-term strategy will work.

Then there are some practical things you can do. Look at your own compensation system, your executive compensation system, and your measurement systems and pension plans. Look at your banks and how you can stimulate them to move the markets in the right direction. It's going to take effort from all of us to move things at this scale if we want to create a brighter future for us and for our children.

If you go on that journey it's very rewarding. One task force I serve on is the Commission for Business and Sustainable Development. It sets out 17 goals that deal with issues such as climate change, poverty alleviation, and gender equality. We have enrolled 1,000 CEOs to wrap sustainable development goals into their business model. If you don't do this, you risk being a dinosaur because your business model will be out of touch with society. Your tenure as a CEO will be short, and your company's lifespan will be short.

We have an opportunity to create a system that works for everybody. We want to eradicate poverty, to attack the issue of climate change, and to make business more equitable. Why wouldn't we all want to be part of that? Why would we just want to make a shareholder rich, and not invest in the future of our planet and of our children?

Chapter 4

Verizon's Multibillion Dollar Bet

Any CEO who wants to make a big long-term capital bet must quickly and effectively explain that strategy to win over investors. Here's how former Verizon CEO Ivan Seidenberg did it.

> *The buy-side stock analysts had an incentive to spend the time to learn our long-term strategy because they were big holders of our stock.*
> —Ivan Seidenberg, former chairman and CEO of Verizon

Over his 10-year tenure as CEO of the giant New York–based telecom Verizon, Ivan Seidenberg totally transformed his old-line telephone company into two businesses—the mobile giant Verizon Wireless and FIOS, a broadband fiber-optic network. He did it at a time when others in his industry were consolidating, slashing costs, and bowing to calls from Wall Street analysts to treat their businesses like cash cows. As analysts pushed for ever-higher dividends and stock buybacks, Seidenberg plowed ahead, investing $150 billion into the company over the course of the decade, which was $25 to $30 billion more than the company would have spent over that same period if it had stuck to its historical rate of capital spending. It was a bold move—and it paid off. Today, Verizon is the second-largest telecom company in the world, boasting both the best wireless network[42] and the highest customer satisfaction in the business wireline industry, according to the research firm J.D. Power.[43]

Any CEO who tries to do what Seidenberg did knows that building out a new business or radically improving a company's products or services does not happen overnight. Such dramatic moves typically require lots of capital spending, and that can depress earnings in the short term, in some cases taking two, three, or more years before the benefits hit the bottom line.

The point is that true strategic change takes time, and certain factions on Wall Street don't have the patience to see such transitions through. How often have we seen a small but influential segment of the investing community challenge a CEO's long-term strategy by pressing for a faster payback or arguing that the free cash would be better spent on higher dividends or stock repurchases than on building up the company for the future? Over the past few decades this kind of pressure has grown. In part, it derives from the rise of the activist investors seeking quick paybacks on their investments, the ever-increasing velocity of capital, a financial news media cycle that runs 24/7 (think Jim Cramer's *Mad Money*), and public policy that does little to incentivize a company to invest for the long term.

One symptom of this rampant short-termism is the record rise of corporate stock buybacks. According to HSBC, companies in the S&P 500 bought back an unprecedented $2.1 trillion of their own shares between 2010 and 2015.[44] Of course, if a CEO has no better place to invest the company's money, there's nothing wrong with giving it back to shareholders. As Warren Buffett wrote in his 2016 Berkshire Hathaway shareholders letter: "As the subject of repurchases has come to a boil, some people have come close to calling them un-American—characterizing them as corporate misdeeds that divert funds needed for productive endeavors. That simply isn't the case: Both American corporations and private investors are today awash in funds looking to be sensibly deployed. I'm not aware of any enticing project that in recent years has died for lack of capital. (Call us if you have a candidate.)"[45]

Buffett has a good point—there's nothing wrong with returning capital to shareholders when the situation warrants. CEOs, however, run into trouble when they decide that their best path is to spend most of their capital on the future of the business, and Wall Street drives down their stock for doing so—in effect punishing them for not buying back *more* stock and not raising the dividend *enough*. Often, public opinion weighs hard on CEOs who have the courage to invest in innovation, skilled workforces, or the essential capital expenditures necessary to sustain long-term growth. Some, in fact, become the target of impatient investors who want their head. According to the consultancy PWC, 17% of the 2,500 largest public companies in the world changed their CEO in 2015, more than in any of the previous 16 years.[46] Many of them, we can imagine, were the victims of impatient investors and boards.

What's to be done to protect a CEO from such short-term pressures? BlackRock CEO Larry Fink, whose investment firm manages more than $6 *trillion* on behalf of clients, believes better communication is a key factor. Each year he writes a letter to the CEOs of the leading companies in which BlackRock's clients are shareholders, discussing how companies can achieve long-term growth in the context of the most recent economic, social, and geopolitical trends. In 2015 Fink wrote: "It is critical . . . to understand that corporate leaders' duty of care and loyalty is not to every investor or trader who owns their companies' shares at any moment in time, but to the company and its long-term owners. Successfully fulfilling that duty requires that corporate leaders engage with a company's long-term providers of capital; that they resist the pressure of short-term shareholders to extract value from the company if it would compromise value creation for long-term owners; and, most importantly, that they clearly and effectively articulate their strategy for sustainable long-term growth."[47]

Cultivate the Right Investors

As Fink suggests, the best defense against short-term market pressures is the ability of CEOs to clearly express their long-term strategy and goals and to explain what short-term sacrifices must be taken to adapt to changing markets and competitors. One of the best examples of a

CEO who successfully resisted short-term Wall Street pressures by skillfully communicating his plans for massive, long-term capital investments is Ivan Seidenberg of Verizon.

Key to Seidenberg's ability to execute his long-term plan: he gained the trust and backing of a solid slate of 20 or so major long-term investors including BlackRock, State Street, and Vanguard.[48] He won them over by creating clear metrics that defined success for his long-term strategy and then met with every one of them at least once a year to explain Verizon's progress against those measures. "We had a point of view of what we thought was good for our industry and the company," says Seidenberg, "and we did not ever want to lose control of our business and allow outsiders to tell us how to run our company. It's not just a matter of bullying your way through. You have to have insights and a sophistication about your industry and the ability to clearly communicate that to your investors. At the same time, you have to produce a sufficient level of results that keep giving you a license to invest for the long."[49]

When Seidenberg became CEO in 2000 the telecom industry was being disrupted. Verizon, which had just been born out of a merger between Bell Atlantic and GTE, ran a nationwide wireless and a landline phone business. By that point, it was becoming increasingly clear that mobile phones would replace landlines and that broadband cable—with the capacity to deliver TV, internet, and voice—would become an important market. Verizon essentially faced two stark choices. It could heed the call of Wall Street, cut costs, watch the rest of the world pass it, and eventually sell itself off. Or it could make bold bets on wireless and cable. Seidenberg chose the latter course.

Pick the Right Metric and Hammer It Home

Making huge, long-term capital bets comes with a special burden on CEOs to bring their key constituencies with them on the journey. After all, you can tell employees what to do, but you can't make investors buy your stock. This is where storytelling becomes vital. To gain support from the investment community, CEOs need to formulate a crystal-clear, compelling business case and then find ways to communicate it to investors in a way that convinces them that going long is worth the wait. Investment managers are among the hardest-hitting, most skeptical people in the world. They want to know where your company is going and whether to take a ride with you. As in politics, voters want lower taxes and more jobs, but they also want a narrative from the White House about where the country is going.

Seidenberg's saga makes this especially clear. During his early days as CEO, the strategy of most players in the telecom industry was simple: Buy smaller telecoms, achieve synergies in operations, and pass the savings back to the shareholders in the form of dividends. Many on Wall Street loved this strategy because the cost savings from such acquisitions provided investors with certainty about where shareholder money was going. Verizon was making its fair share of acquisitions and accruing cash from the synergies, but Seidenberg had other plans for that capital.

Despite pressure from the Wall Street to raise dividends or buy back more stock, the CEO decided to invest a good portion of that money back into the business and still pay a generous dividend. "We had a view that over the long term having a quality network was a competitive advantage," says Seidenberg. "We had competitors that bragged about how low their capital expenses were and eventually those companies did not compete very well and ended up having to sell off their business."

Seidenberg says that he did two things absolutely religiously that helped get his board and some of his biggest shareholders on his side. First, he rigorously courted long-term investors. Second, he told his directors and investors that what he really cared about was expanding market share, which would lead to higher revenue growth, and that the way to achieve that was to build the best quality networks.

The building of Verizon's wireless network had the biggest impact on growth. In all, Seidenberg invested around $110 billion in wireless, buying spectrum licenses from the government, snapping up a string of other cellular companies, and spending heavily in new, powerful technologies. In 2010, Verizon launched its 4G LTE (fourth-generation Long Term Evolution) mobile broadband network, the most advanced 4G network in the United States, in 38 major metropolitan areas. By 2015, Verizon's 4G LTE network provided coverage for approximately 312 million people across the nation.

Seidenberg also took aim at the cable industry. At that time, most competitors were installing copper-coaxial line in the home to deliver TV, phone, and internet access. Verizon offered only "dial-up" internet access on its telephone lines and no TV service. To compete, Seidenberg knew he'd have to offer a better, faster product. This involved laying fiber-optic cable to the "last mile" into the customer's home—a huge and expensive undertaking. In 2004 Verizon announced it would install a million fiber-optic lines at a cost of $23 billion in a new service called FIOS. Many on Wall Street weren't happy with the news.[50]

Remember Not All Investors Are Created Equal

When dealing with the investment community, the CEO must remember that investors are not a homogenous class. An activist such as Nelson Peltz can have a different agenda than an activist such as Third Point's Daniel Loeb, and those two may have wildly different philosophies than, say, a big investor such as Fidelity or State Street. The key is to cultivate those major shareholders who are really long-term shareholders. Think of it as marketing your stock like you market your product. As with all good marketing campaigns, you have to have a compelling product, a sexy story, and a persuasive strategy—in other words, it has to make big investors lean forward, buy, and hold.

When Seidenberg started selling his plan to invest heavily in wireless and broadband, most of the resistance came from the "sell-side" analysts, Wall Street researchers who rate and recommend stocks to clients based on their near-term growth potential. The primary role of America's roughly 6,000 sell-side analysts[51] who work at the globe's 12 largest banks is to advise their clients on investment opportunities. In general, they create value by generating insights about a company's business over the next few quarters, providing analysis on performance, short-term market trends, and the competition. Their role is to direct their customers—often hedge funds, managed mutual funds, and other investors who favor short-term trading—to buy or sell the stock today, not to predict how it will do 10 years from now. In the investing world, sell-side analysts play a different role than "buy-side" analysts, who work for big institutional investors such as pension funds, asset managers, and university endowments that tend to buy and hold shares of a company for the long term.

Seidenberg soon discovered that it wasn't worth his time to try to get sell-side analysts to buy into his long-term vision. "I ended up delegating conversations with the sell-side to my team. I didn't go out of my way to court them because I always felt they had multiple agendas. They owned our stock or didn't own it, they were covering other industries or covering our suppliers or our competitors." In other words, Seidenberg felt that the advice he was getting from the sell side wasn't always in the best long-term interests of his business. He adds: "This is a core issue about short versus long management. If companies get conflicted advice about the long and short term, they won't make good decisions."

For example, Verizon's wireless business was doing well, but Seidenberg recalls how the sell side was fixated on the troubled landline division and questioned how much he was investing in FIOS. "Even when we had reduced land lines to only 20% of the company, that's all the sell side wanted to call me up and talk about." From 2004 to 2006 Seidenberg was spending heavily to build out his FIOS fiber-optic network and to bolster his mobile business, and he acquired the wireless carrier MCI for $6.8 billion. The sell side didn't like the direction Verizon was moving in, and the stock dropped from $48 when he took over Verizon in 2000 to around $25 in late 2005. "People were saying, 'Ivan, you're crazy,'" recalls Seidenberg.

"But we had a vision for the future and knew what this investment would produce in the long term."

Realizing that the sell side didn't care for his long-term strategy, Seidenberg decided to win over the buy-side analysts. Because they owned large positions in Verizon, buy-side investors such as Capital Research and State Street were willing to go deep on what the company was doing and, says Seidenberg, asked smart questions. Seidenberg met with 5 of his top 20 investors at the end of each quarter so that by year's end he would have met with all of them at least once. "If you take the time with them," says Seidenberg, "the buy side can understand the long-term story."

Seidenberg worked hard to prove to the Wall Street that the incremental capital Verizon was spending was resulting in market share gains. At every board meeting and investor presentation he would show whether deployed capital would generate growth in the short term, the medium term, or the long term. "Obviously everyone says they do this," says Seidenberg, "but we were different because we were really very open about looking at the competition. We used to dissect our competitors at every board meeting. What were they doing and how were they cleaning our clock? What were the cable companies doing to us or what was Apple's iPhone doing to us? We had a very sophisticated process to let our board and our investors know that our future revenue streams are being eaten alive."

In the mid-2000s, for example, Verizon knew it had to update its mobile system to keep growing market share. However, it would take three or four years to deploy all the technology for its high-speed 4G network. Seidenberg explained to the buy side why 4G was necessary to keep Verizon competitive and grow market share, but he was also careful not to link his earnings plan to his growth plan. He would tell the buy side that the company was going to try to mine value out of everything it did. "I never said to them," recalls Seidenberg, "that our earnings would be bad for two years and then be better in the third year. That would just confuse things."

To stress his focus on the long term, Seidenberg in 2006 stopped offering earnings guidance. "I got hammered. The sell side was whining and crying like crazy: 'What are you hiding? Why are you doing it? You can't do that to us.' The buy side thought it was hilarious because they knew enough about our business that they could generate their own earnings numbers."

In the end Seidenberg couldn't control what the buy side or sell side did, but what he could control was his own destiny. His market-share metrics, his competitive analysis, and a rising stream of earnings from the $150 billion he invested in wireless and telecom gave his long-term strategy time to bear fruit. In 2011, as part of a smoothly orchestrated transition, Seidenberg handed the company over to his lieutenant, Lowell McAdam, who continued to pursue the company's long-term strategy of offering among the best products and services in its field.

Executive Summary
Capital Investments for Going Long

1. Going long sometimes requires huge capital investments—it's incredibly expensive. Verizon CEO Seidenberg spent a staggering $150 billion in total on his telecom and broadband networks.
2. CEOs need a clear and compelling business case that their top team, employees, and investors can back with enthusiasm. In Seidenberg's case, it was to create the best products and services in the telecommunications industry and then support that strategy through capital spending.
3. In terms of winning over investors, it helps to pick a clear, easy-to-understand metric as a defining element of long-term growth. Seidenberg picked market-share growth to show his investors that his long-term strategy was on track. Of course, every market is different. In some industries, for example, you can pick up market share by cutting prices, but that might not do you any good in the long run. Pick a metric that works best for your market.
4. CEOs need to remember that not all investors are alike. Short-term traders won't go with you but plenty of long-term investors will if you can reach out and persuade them to take the journey with you.

Advice from Ivan Seidenberg to Other CEOs

When I retired, my parting comment to my board was I always felt that we had a point of view about our industry, about how to serve customers, and how to achieve market-share growth. Any CEO who wants to manage for the long term should know their company, customers, and industry as well as anyone, and they have to really demonstrate a firm grasp of the markets they're operating in and a realistic understanding of their position—and then articulate a plan. They need to hire people who really know their markets and can create best-in-class products and services. I wanted our wireless and landline people, for example, not to focus on whether we're bundling three products like video, voice, and data or giving someone a discount on the bill. I wanted to make sure we had the best products inside the bundles. Too often CEOs with their CFO will focus on a financial plan rather than a long-term plan. You have to make those two things come together. It's hard but if you work at it, it can be done.

Market share to me is an extraordinarily important metric. If someone hired me tomorrow to run a company I'd say, "Give me a list of all products and services and look at market share trends and how your competitors are doing and I would want to know what the trends are in terms of market share—are you gaining or losing market share and why?" And I would really focus on whether we had the right products to compete. From that I would develop a long-term strategy. Do we need to sell stuff, buy stuff? Do we need to invest, acquire, or not acquire? And then, from there, do we need to start investing capital?

You also need to take great pains to be transparent with the board and your long-term investors. You need to discuss the risks and rewards and let them know that you're not sitting back, but willing to take risks, and that you really intend to change the arc of existence. Every company says they're doing it, but most aren't. You have to constantly stay ahead of the curve.

Chapter 5

R&D Is the Last Place to Cut

Despite calls from investors to cut research spending, 3M CEO George Buckley kept everyone happy by finding other sources of savings and plowing them back into future products.

You get better results not by squeezing the lemon but by planting more lemon groves.
—Sir George Buckley, former CEO of 3M

When Sir George Buckley assumed the chairman and CEO role at 3M in 2005, he found a company that had long been known for innovation—it had created Scotch tape, Post-it Notes, and thousands of other consumer and industrial products over its proud 100+ year history. He also found a company that was suffering from sluggish growth and had just gone through severe layoffs and a bout of cost cutting. In the four years before he arrived, capital spending had been slashed by 65% and R&D by 25%. Earnings had indeed improved under Buckley's predecessor, but the newly installed CEO was worried about the future.

Buckley, a straight-talking Brit who grew up under tough circumstances in the slum area of Pitsmoor, in Sheffield, England, is an engineer by training—and, he says, by inclination. He displays an uncanny knack of driving straight to the heart of a problem and inspiring people to rise to the occasion to solve it. But the executive team and workforce he says he encountered when he arrived at 3M were demoralized and scarred by years of cutbacks. How could he get them to rekindle their imagination, take more risks, and become more innovative again?

Companies looking to build a strong R&D culture first tailor what is measured, monitored, and controlled to suit their long-term outcomes and then strike the right balance between performance and innovation. When Buckley asked himself why 3M wasn't enjoying solid growth, he discovered that the board and the former leaders had not made the natural link between innovation and growth and had been solely focused on classical financial metrics: EPS growth and economic value added, a measurement of how efficiently the company deployed its capital. The root of the problem, as Buckley saw it, was that in the name of short-term results, innovation (and the growth that came along with it) was being shortchanged. In addition, the company's scientists and engineers had been made to feel like second-class citizens.

Buckley reached back into 3M's history and reinstated a key metric known as the New Product Vitality Index (NPVI). He examined the decline of 3M's core businesses and found that, just to overcome natural attrition, at least 14% of the company's revenues must come from products introduced in the last five years. "No one in the company knew these numbers anymore," recalls the CEO. "They should have been front and central to them, but they had fallen into disuse."[52] But this 14% only holds the company's year-over-year growth flat. To grow at a 4% compounded annual growth rate above what the market was growing required a NPVI in excess of 30%.

Through this lens Buckley saw that 3M's core products were dying—some were being attacked by the competition, while others were cannibalized by new products. He found that only 8%—nevermind 30%—of the revenues in the company's core business were coming from products introduced in the previous five years. Some important divisions' NPVIs were even zero, where new product development and innovation had been completely eliminated. That meant 3M's core product lines were wasting away faster than new product lines could replace them. Says Buckley: "Once I showed my team the numbers I'd derived, there was a 'holy shit' reaction. So I said, 'Look guys, we've got to get back to innovating and growth. Because when you're growing at 1% and the market is growing at 3%—this is not going to have a happy ending.'"

Buckley took another extraordinary step to rebuild 3M. For many years 3M's engineers and scientists had been allowed to spend 15% of their time (roughly a day per week) inventing and developing whatever products they wanted to—not those directed by the company. Of course, that cost money, but this arrangement had produced many successful products over the years, including the legendary Post-it Notes. The 15% "free time" program had been eliminated a few years earlier in a drive to make R&D more efficient. Buckley was appalled on hearing this a few weeks after arriving at 3M, and to spur creativity and innovation he immediately reinstated it.

By the time he took mandatory retirement at age 65 in 2012, Buckley had grown the share of new products launched over the previous five years from 8% of sales to 34% of sales. And if you look at the company's performance over the long haul, 3M's stock from the time Buckley took the helm in late 2005 to 2017 (his lieutenant became CEO and continued his long-term strategy) has more than tripled.

Know Short-Termism Hurts Innovation

What Buckley knew from previous experience was that you can't compete in today's environment without spurring cutting-edge R&D. Read the business section of your favorite newspaper or download the latest issue of *McKinsey Quarterly* and you're likely to find an insightful article about how technology is disrupting industry after industry. As we all well know, the rise of big data, next-generation analytics, artificial intelligence, the Internet of Things, and robotics is turning multiple sectors of the global economy upside down. Taxi medallions in New York City not so long ago sold for $1 million each. Since Uber arrived on the scene with its on-demand car service, the value of a medallion as of late 2017 had fallen to $186,000.[53] The online home-sharing service Airbnb has the hotel industry scrambling for new ways to lure back lost customers. A decade ago, Wal-Mart was the king of retailing, dominating the business headlines. Now, Amazon, through its shrewd use of technology, is grabbing up market share at a dizzying rate.

Managing disruptive technology has become a matter of life and death for big business. According to the consultancy Innosight, the average tenure of a company listed on the S&P 500 stock index in 1965 was 33 years. Today, it is 18 years—and that number is forecasted to shrink to 14 years by 2026.[54] That would mean that half the S&P 500 companies currently on the list will get pushed off over the next decade by a bevy of young and hungry usurpers.

All this disruption also means that over the next decade there will be a heightened premium on innovation. To compete, more established companies will need to spend a great deal of capital to constantly keep their products and services a step ahead of their rivals'. The challenge is that some investors on Wall Street would rather see CEOs spend their capital not on R&D but rather on higher dividends or stock buybacks. A study looking at businesses targeted by activists found that their median expenditures for R&D basically stalled while those for a random sample of firms increased by more than 20% over the same period of years.[55] As you can imagine, many of the CEOs who led those firms likely shrank their R&D spending largely because of the chilling effect caused by being targeted by aggressive activists.

And it's not only the activists who are clamoring for less R&D. Some institutional investors are not sure investments in basic R&D are worth the wait. According to Columbia Law School professor John Coffee, Jr., and Rutgers professor Darius Palia in their study *The Wolf at the Door: The Impact of Hedge Fund Activism on Corporate Governance*, after the financial crisis of 2008 some institutional investors—wanting to make up for heavy losses in the stock market—funneled money to hedge funds that pressed for quick returns.[56] That, among other things, increased pressure on CEOs to cut R&D spending. That, quite simply, was wrongheaded. As legendary

Sony CEO Akio Morita put it: "To gain profit is important, but you must invest to build up assets that you can cash in in the future."[57]

Of course, it's relatively easy to buck Wall Street and spend appropriate amounts of capital on R&D if you're cash rich. Apple, which as of 2017 had $257 billion in cash on hand,[58] has come under fire from activist Carl Icahn. Even so, it spends whatever it takes to make the iPhone a technological leader. Alphabet, which in late 2017 had $100 billion in cash,[59] hired itself an activist-savvy chief financial officer (CFO) in Ruth Porat. She was previously CFO of Morgan Stanley, which fended off activist investor Dan Loeb of Third Point Capital.[60] In the meantime, Alphabet continually improves Google's search algorithms while spending on basic research projects from self-driving cars to kites that generate wind electricity.[61]

But what about companies that don't have that kind of cash? How can you as a CEO or top leader find the funds when investors are clamoring for short-term gains?

Find the Money Elsewhere

3M's George Buckley is a case in point. As we've noted, when he became CEO the company was suffering from sluggish growth and had just gone through severe layoffs and cost cutting. Any CEO looking to innovate needs to find the right balance between short-term returns and long-term investing. It's unrealistic to think that in this age of rampant short-termism investors will grant a CEO license to shave earnings and dividends for a payoff that might be 5 to 10 years in the future. So if Buckley was to get 3M to reach his goal of getting at least 30% of each division's revenues from products introduced in the last five years—he knew he would have to find the money to fund R&D without diluting earnings. He did two things: He freed up capital by reshaping his portfolio of businesses and also by making his supply chain and operations more efficient.

At the time 3M had a pharmaceutical business that was absorbing a large chunk of the company's R&D budget. The problem with the pharmaceutical industry, as Buckley saw it, was that it followed what he calls the Rule of Nine. "You have nine programs going simultaneously, you spend $900 million on them, each one takes nine years to complete, and then the FDA takes nine years to approve them and only one in nine is successful. That's not innovation; that's gambling," he said.

So Buckley and his team sold off the pharmaceutical business in 2007 for $2.1 billion, which gave him some room to increase R&D spending from 2% of revenues to 4% of revenues. Next, he tackled 3M's vast global supply chain, which not only freed up more money for R&D but also improved customer service in the process. When Buckley looked under the hood he found that the average time from raw material to finished goods was 180 days—very high for any kind of manufacturing. Only 73% of the company's products were being delivered to customers on time. "The only ones who will buy from you when your fulfillment rates are so bad," says Buckley, "are those who have no other choice, those who aren't coming back, or those who aren't going to pay."

While analyzing the working capital problem, Buckley discovered that some products moved to as many as seven locations—from Canada to Germany and Germany to Belgium and then back to Alabama, Illinois, and so on—before ending up in a customer's hands. It was like a seething anthill of stuff moving all over the world. Products got shunted around from country to country during the manufacturing process solely based on available manufacturing capacity. The goal had been to keep the in-plant unit manufacturing cost down, but the strategy also resulted in slow deliveries and high transportation and logistics costs. Huge amounts of working capital were being consumed in this process.

Buckley corrected the issue by mandating that products in the top 30 supply chains could not move plants more than once. This entailed moving several production lines from one plant to another, closing a few facilities, and opening 18 new ones in geographic areas that made more sense from a growth perspective. By doing so he was able to boost working capital in the first year of his reengineering initiative from $635 million to more than $1.2 billion and, additionally, improve delivery times dramatically. Most of the extra money would flow directly into R&D.

Listen to the Rank and File

Now Buckley had to decide where to spend his R&D war chest. When deciding where to invest R&D, CEOs typically give the most money to the biggest, most successful divisions in their companies. The problem with this approach, however, is that the CEO might end up starving a promising young business. Such a strategy also creates a culture of winners and losers within the corporation, breeding resentment and jealousy in those who end up with paltry R&D budgets. A better approach is for the CEO to apply zero-based budgeting to R&D, allocating funds based on how well the division heads make a case for research dollars, no matter how small their business.

This gambit worked particularly well at 3M. Most people think of 3M as a single huge corporation, but it is actually made up of 37 different reporting companies focused on everything from adhesives to electronics to automotive parts and more. The challenge in a situation like this is that if you have, like 3M, a collection of businesses that are generating $50 million, $100 million, or $700 million a year in revenues, no single business has enough volume to affect the overall sales growth of the company—the arithmetic just doesn't work. So your only option is to try to innovate and grow *everywhere*.

Buckley and CFO Pat Campbell listened to the input offered by the leaders and employees of their 37 divisions. Each was asked to put together a one-page business plan to talk about new product and growth potential, as well as the split between capital expenditure and how much they wanted to spend on expenses, R&D included. Then the duo ranked them based on the quality of their ideas and on their historical growth rates in sales and earnings.

But getting new R&D money had a catch. Buckley applied a metric he called a "leveraged ratio" to the growth numbers. This is how it worked: If a business had the same earnings and sales growth rate it would have a leveraged ratio of 1. For example, if sales were growing at 4% and earnings at 6%, the business would have a ratio of 1.5%, which is good because it means margins are being enhanced by growth. If the ratio is under 1, however, it means margins are being eroded by growth. To win R&D money at 3M, a business needed to first have a leveraged ratio of *at least* 1. By forcing people to hit a leveraged ratio of 1 or more, Buckley created yet another bucket of money he could use for R&D.

Of course, a CEO needs to be both disciplined and flexible. In some cases, Buckley was open to proposals that didn't meet the established criteria. "Once in a while a division would come to us with the proverbial tin cup and bleeding hearts and said they can't get there unless they got some money now," he said. If their case was compelling enough, and their project attractive, they would get R&D money.

Nurture an Innovation Culture

Money is a necessary but not entirely sufficient means to spur innovation in organizations. CEOs must create a culture where people feel they are not only supported by the executive team but also safe to take risks and perhaps even fail. For the first six months Buckley was CEO, he didn't receive a single idea for growth from his 37 divisions. "They were still fearful of failure and that their project would get killed stone dead—and so might they," he recalls. He sent a clear message that if you failed, it was not necessarily the end of the world or your career. He believed strongly that some failure is a natural part of a creative culture.

The leveraged ratio screen Buckley and his CFO used provided an additional benefit besides just raising cash for R&D. It sent a signal throughout the organization that corporate was not picking winners and losers. Whether you worked in 3M's biggest or smallest division, you had a shot at getting increased R&D and growth funding. And once people started realizing that projects they had been afraid for years to propose might get funding, a floodgate of ideas opened. During his first year in the job the number of ideas increased from none to 60. By the end of the second year the executive team had twice as many good ideas as it could fund without affecting operating margins. And employee engagement numbers had risen significantly—at the end of his tenure, they had risen by a factor of five.

Even during the financial crisis that hit in 2008, Buckley kept true to his strategy, believing that no matter how bad things got in the short term he should keep his focus on the long run. Most notably, he didn't cut R&D spending—not by one dollar. This sent another important message. His employees saw that he was actually doing what he said he was going to do—consistently boost innovation—even through a heart-wrenching downturn.

One of the most successful products that came out of Buckley's push for innovation was a new kind of abrasive paper called Cubitron II. At his first quarterly business review Buckley said to the head of his abrasives division, "Tell me what's new in abrasives."

The manager looked at him and said, "We don't think of our business like that. We see it as a low growth, low margin, manage for cash business."

The CEO replied: "I know less than 10% of what you know about abrasives, but I think they are sexy." Then he quipped: "Yes, I know, maybe I need to get out more. But everything you see in this room—the loom that made the carpet, the dry wall, the wood tabletop, my eye glasses—were all made either directly or indirectly with abrasives."

Buckley, who often likes to think about how nature would solve a problem, then asked whether an abrasive grain could be shaped like a shark's tooth, one of the sharpest natural materials in the world. The R&D team later said they had had that idea before and no one gave them money to explore it. Buckley asked how much it would take to make a prototype of a shark-tooth-shaped abrasive. The answer: a couple of months and a couple of million. He said to do it.

Eventually, 3M's engineers found a way to place the shark-tooth-shaped grains upright on a substrate to maximize its cutting potential. The new product, Cubitron II, which launched in 2009,[62] cuts five times faster and lasts five times longer than conventional abrasives. Before Cubitron II, the abrasives division had 1% revenue growth, 11% margins, and a 13% return on invested capital. When Buckley left the company, it had 28% revenue growth, 28% margins, and a 34% return on invested capital. Says Buckley: "This is how the power of innovation can work in what many saw as a moribund business."

Seek Innovation in the Everyday

Any CEO wanting to spur innovation should understand that there can be as much gain in improving processes and materials as there is in new product launches. In other words, innovation can be about not just adding technology but doing something you used to do at a fraction of the cost. 3M, for example, is the largest respiratory mask maker in the world. At a strategic planning meeting Buckley asked what it cost to make each mask. He was told it cost over a dollar. So he then challenged the leader of that division to make one for just five cents.

She looked at Buckley from the other side of the table and said, "George, it's impossible"—the cost of the material alone, she said, was vastly more than five cents. Over the next six months this highly talented manager, believing the task was impossible, put Buckley off. He then told her that if she was not going to rise to the occasion, he'd give the project to another division. That did the trick—she knew he was serious. She took up the challenge with gusto, seeking innovative ways to cut material, change the design (she got rid of the aluminum strip over the nose), and make the manufacturing process and supply chain more efficient. A year later, 3M released a mask to market that cost less than 10 cents to make.

"There's not a product in the world you can't innovate," says Buckley. "Just use your imagination, laud successes, and ignore some of the failures, and this will change people's attitudes to the point where they start to think they can really do this."

And at 3M, they did.

Executive Summary
R&D Investments Are Key to Going Long

1. When the economy gets tough or an activist targets a company, R&D spending is often one of the first places to take a hit. CEOs looking to invest in the products and services that will pay off 5 or 10 years down the road must find ways to protect their R&D budget. 3M's George Buckley found capital for R&D by spinning off a pharmaceutical business and streamlining his manufacturing process.

2. CEOs may also make the mistake of giving the most R&D money to their biggest, most successful divisions. The problem with this approach is that the CEO might end up starving a promising young business, or perhaps create a culture of winners and losers within the corporation, breeding resentment and jealousy. Buckley, by contrast, applied a zero-based budgeting strategy to R&D, allocating funds based on how well the division heads made a case for research dollars, no matter how small their business.

3. Money is necessary but not sufficient to spur innovation in organizations. CEOs must create a culture where people feel they are not only supported by the executive team but also feel safe to take risks and fail.

4. Any CEO wanting to spur innovation should understand that there can be as much gain in improving processes and materials as there is in new product launches. In other words, innovation can be about not just adding technology but doing something you used to do at a fraction of the cost.

Advice from Sir George Buckley to Other CEOs

The core of every company is dying. Core products are dying because they are being continuously attacked by competition, by new technology, by cannibalization, and by regulations. That means you have to innovate to survive. But figuring out how and when to innovate is one of the great challenges of life. What you have to keep in mind is that it's worth all the trouble because innovation spurs growth and growth is almost always the greatest wealth creator for the shareholder.

If you're in a 3% market, unless you do something to actively intervene you're only going to grow at 3% or less. So you need to spend

(continued)

money on innovation. Look at your toughest competitor and ask yourself: "Can I out-procure them? Can I deploy capital better? Can I outsell or out-market them?" The answer is probably no. The only way to beat them is to outthink them and that's innovation.

Innovation is nonlinear and takes a lot of time. A new industrial product can take 15 years or more before reaching its full market potential. And it takes lots of capital. Find money in other parts of the company to fund R&D so you don't have to take a hit on earnings. Look at divesting businesses, improving logistics, or rationalizing your supply chain to free up a pot of gold for investing in the future.

Then you have to encourage people to take risks and deal creatively with uncertainty. The most important job of any leader is to give your employees hope. Samuel Johnson once said, "Without hope there can be no endeavor." You have to show people a plausible and defensible dream and with your actions show them you believe in them. You have to get them to believe in a greater good. And that greater good is investing for the long term. In other words, you get better results not by squeezing the lemon but by planting more lemon groves.

Chapter 6

Boards That Think Long

CEOs who want to go long need directors who get deeply involved in setting a strategy.

The idea was that if an activist was writing a letter to HPE demanding incremental shareholder value, what would it say?
—Maggie Wilderotter, director of HPE

L ike most directors, Maggie Wilderotter hopes to never face a nasty attack by an activist investor. Wilderotter, who sits on the boards of Hewlett Packard Enterprise (HPE) and Costco, worked with her fellow directors at HPE on an unusual exercise to avoid that very situation. They composed a letter to management as if it had been written by an activist, asking for a radical change in strategy, and then worked with CEO Meg Whitman to shape and implement it. As a result, HPE made a huge strategic pivot.

Wilderotter represents a new (but rare) breed of director who is taking a deeper and more active role in strategy. We believe that CEOs should encourage this kind of behavior on their boards. In this fast-moving world, any CEO who wishes to go long needs the help of seasoned directors whose experience can help them make the right long-term decisions.

For as long as corporations have existed, the primary role of a board has been to look out for the interests of the shareholder. In fact, in the United States today, directors by law must put the needs of stockholders ahead of any other constituencies. Directors do this by making sure they have a strong set of governance laws in place, by hiring the right CEO for the job, and by creating financial incentives that align the interests of the executive team with those of the shareholders.

All those duties remain important, but today's directors need to do more. We argue that the twenty-first-century board has two new, distinct responsibilities beyond governance, talent, and compensation. First, today's board needs to get deeply involved with long-term strategy, and second, it must help sell that vision to the company's investors.

A board giving a CEO advice on strategy is nothing new. Typically, however, CEOs formulate a strategy, and then the directors essentially rubber-stamp the plan. The tendency is for directors to play it safe, and not make the tough decisions or take the big risks necessary to sustain the value of an enterprise over the long run. As activist Carl Icahn once put it at a commencement speech at Drexel University: "I sit on a lot of boards. . . . I don't have to watch *Saturday Night Live* anymore, I just sit at the board meetings. I will tell you it's a sad commentary that we have an inability to compete. You can blame unions to some extent. But with some exceptions the real problem is that . . . there's a symbiotic relationship between boards and CEOs today. And as a result, there is no way to hold these guys accountable except when someone like myself comes along or some other person who is really willing to challenge them. But you have to go through contortions. There is no corporate democracy."[63]

A recent study on what keeps a board from being a high-performing one identified five elements, one of which was a "lack of alignment and agreement on company strategy." The report found that confusion over a company's strategy caused disinterest among board members, who then simply default to tackling regulatory and compliance issues. As the report concluded: "This often causes board disruption and sends damaging signals to financial markets."[64]

If you look at what separates a strong performing company from a poor performing one, it's hard to find much difference between the makeup of the boards, the experience of the directors, how many times they meet each year, and how much they get paid. How, then, can a board make a difference? Again, we believe it's the willingness of directors to get more involved in their company's long-term strategy. Most CEOs don't like this notion, believing that strategy is the purview of management. But CEOs who walk the high-wire act of going long could use the wisdom and backing of board members who deeply understand the company's strategy, can engage in give-and-take with the executive team, solve difficult problems together, and show mutual respect for one another.

The world has gotten too complicated and events are changing too fast for CEOs to handle big strategic challenges on their own. The retailing sector is under assault by Amazon, the publishing sector by Facebook and Google, and the automotive sector by Tesla; the list only goes on and on. These are massive and very difficult shifts. If CEOs are to set and execute long-term strategies that successfully address such challenges, they need active directors who have knowledge of the industry, understand emerging technologies, know how to build talent, and can and will get involved with the work of defining the company's future. Once the strategy is set, it then becomes the responsibility of directors to help the CEO sell that vision to investors.

Develop Directors Who Dig Deep

To find out how this new breed of director works in practice, we spoke with Maggie Wilderotter, who not only has experience as a CEO—she ran the telecom company Frontier Communications from 2004 to early 2015—but currently sits on the public company boards of Costco, HPE, Cadence Design Systems, and Juno Therapeutics, a bio-pharmaceutical start-up. She also serves on the boards of several private companies including Tanium, a maker of cybersecurity software, Chobani, and Cakebread Cellars. On top of that, she operates her own boutique luxury inn on her vineyard in Amador County, California.

Wilderotter points to computer giant HPE as a good example of a board that takes an active role in setting strategy. After splitting Hewlett Packard into two businesses in 2015 (the printer and ink business became HP, and the enterprise computing business became HPE), CEO Meg Whitman stayed on to run the new enterprise group. She faced huge strategic challenges. After the spinoff, what remained was a large collection of enterprise businesses with $70 billion in annual sales that built and sold computer servers, and provided business software and consulting services in a highly competitive market. HPE was at an inflection point and needed to be repositioned if it was to have a bright future. Says Wilderotter, who joined the HPE board after the split: "The HPE business units were not synergistic; they were in highly competitive environments and all needed investments. HPE was more like a holding company than an operating company."[65]

To help crystalize a new long-term strategy for HPE, the board conducted an unusual exercise. In 2015, it composed a letter to management as if an activist had written it. Says Wilderotter: "The idea was that if an activist was writing a letter to HPE demanding incremental shareholder value, what would it say?" Wilderotter says that CEO Whitman backed the idea from the start and that the exercise helped the board take a close look in the mirror and decide which businesses HPE should be in and which it should not.

The exercise worked in large part because the board was made up of experienced tech-savvy directors who were willing to debate strategy with the executive team. Besides Wilderotter, HPE's board also included Marc Andreessen, cofounder of a leading Silicon Valley venture capital firm, Andreessen Horowitz, and also a director at Facebook; Ray Lane, who had been president of the software giant Oracle; Ray Ozzie, the former chief software architect at Microsoft; and Gary Reiner, an operating partner at the private equity firm General Atlantic and formerly the chief information officer at GE.

The letter started out with a preamble that recommended a fresh look in the mirror. It stated where the company's real strengths lie, where it wasn't winning, and bold ideas on what HPE should do to create the best value for shareholders.

With that backdrop, the board and management embarked on a full review of the state of the industry and the current portfolio. There were no sacred cows. The result of this process, says Wilderotter, was a recommendation that HPE's focus should be on data center services such as hybrid IT, the intelligent edge including networks and the Internet of Things, and consulting and support services for those business areas.

Businesses such as software and IT operation and business process services should be sold off, it was decided. The company could then, as a result, realize meaningful synergy cost savings. "Our long-term strategy," says Wilderotter, "was to sell businesses that weren't creating value . . . but to keep assets where we had the best capabilities so we could be more focused and could have more sustainability in the long run."

The board dove deep into the details. It looked at the structures of divesting—a basic sale, a cash sale—but ultimately it recommended using Reverse Morris Trusts because it was more tax efficient for shareholders than outright sales.

At first, recalls Wilderotter, some members of Whitman's executive team felt that the plan was too aggressive and too disruptive to the day-to-day business. The board argued back that management was being too conservative and that the ongoing technology revolution was going to happen a lot faster than they thought—and that it was going to be painful.

Wilderotter says that while the board took a leadership role with the CEO on this strategic review, it ended up being a highly collaborative process with the leadership. After lengthy discussion and debate, management and the board aligned. "We did different iterations of the strategic imperatives," recalls Wilderotter, "but once we agreed on what we would do, we locked arms and implemented."

Over the next several months, management sold off HPE's software business for $7.5 billion and its 225,000-person software and IT operation and business process services for $35 billion. The two transactions created an incremental $10.5 billion gain for share-holders. HPE also acquired Aruba, a leader in the Intelligent Edge/Internet of Things business, to help it gain a stronger foothold in this fast-growing segment. As of late 2017 the new HPE—after making a few other "tuck in" acquisitions in the new strategic businesses—was a smaller, more focused technology company, with $35 billion in annual sales. Whitman, who remains on the board, stepped aside as CEO, and her top lieutenant, President Antonio Neri, was chosen by the board to be CEO and execute HPE's new long-term strategy. Says Wilderotter: "It was either become irrelevant or get this company focused on the right strategy. Now we have the assets that give us the best chance to be sustainable in the long run."

There's another upside to this "activist letter" exercise, says Wilderotter. She explains: "If you decide not to do something and you're challenged by investors, it allows you to have a solid argument for what choices the board decided on and what we chose not to do—and why." That's a handy weapon to keep shareholder support intact.

Sell the Vision to Investors

Wilderotter says that the boards she sits on at Costco, Cadence, and Juno Therapeutics get deep into the thickets on strategy, but the directors there also play another important role—selling that strategy to investors. Like every other retailer in America, Costco faces a competitive threat from the titans of retail, Wal-Mart and Amazon. So far Costco is doing the right things right in an ultra-challenging environment. The giant warehouse chain is holding up well, with its stock in 2017 rising 16.5% on strong membership renewals and sales growth. Even despite the success, the board regularly discusses long-term strategy with management. Topics include how to set a robust online strategy, how to balance its warehouse business with its e-commerce sales, and how to attract and retain new and existing customers. The board delves into details such as simplifying Costco's e-commerce site, the online ordering process, partnerships, and new delivery options.

The board discussions are not limited to the competitive environment. Almost since its inception, Costco has focused on building an environmentally sustainable business. The company, says Wilderotter, has long been dedicated to environmental, social, and governance (ESG) principles, and the directors make sure that management keeps moving ahead on this track. Toward that end, Costco is expanding its recycling and efficiency programs. It has humane treatment programs in place for the meat and poultry it sells. It holds its employees and suppliers to ESG standards. "We have a great business model that we've been refining for years and it works," says Wilderotter. "For example, if there is a food recall, we take the food instantaneously off the shelves, clean and sterilize every warehouse, and notify every customer immediately."

While Costco's strategy and its ESG approach seem to be working, many in the investing world don't know the extent of the company's story. That's why a number of directors at the retailer speak with investors and explain how the retailer is doing business. "Some of the investors didn't know Costco operated in this way," says Wilderotter. "Some knew certain business practices, but only to a certain extent. In discussions with investors, we can get them up to speed."

Typically, a company deploys its CFO or uses analysts to talk to institutional investors. Today, as we will discuss in more detail in chapter 8, big asset managers such as BlackRock, State Street, and Vanguard, whose index funds control trillions, are getting more actively involved in the companies in which their funds invest. Because these big asset managers are relatively new at doing this, their stewardship teams, who act as watchdogs for the funds, aren't always that familiar with the ins and outs of the different companies in which they're investing. Wilderotter believes it is also the job of a director—in addition to management—to talk directly to these important investors about how their company is creating long-term shareholder value.

For example, in 2017 Wilderotter traveled to London to attend a conference of investors. She met with many of the big index funds and institutions and explained what Costco was doing about the environment, sustainability, governance, diversity, and pay practices. "Investors are taking ESG issues very seriously these days," she says.

At the London conference, investors also pressed her on how Costco was dealing with pressure from Amazon. She explained to them what Costco was doing to better its performance, providing examples of improvements in e-commerce and explaining the power the private label Kirkland brand offers: high-quality products at low prices. To the surprise of many investors at the conference, she pointed out that while Amazon has its free shipping program, Costco's products, on average, are substantially cheaper than Amazon's. Wilderotter's hope is that her evangelism will help solidify the relationship with long-term investors and lower the number of investors who rotate out of the stock.

Wilderotter's role as a corporate board strategist and evangelist is not easy to pull off—it takes hard work and time—but more directors could certainly help their companies profit by following her lead.

Executive Summary
Get Your Board to Become More Actively Involved

1. The twenty-first-century board has two new, distinct responsibilities beyond governance, talent, and compensation. Today's board needs to get deeply involved with long-term strategy, and it must also help position that strategy to the company's key investors.
2. CEOs who want to go long should seek out the wisdom and backing of board members who deeply understand the company's strategy, can engage in give-and-take with the executive team, can solve difficult problems, and show mutual respect for one another.
3. To help crystalize a new long-term strategy for HPE, the board composed a letter to management as if an activist had written it. Says director Maggie Wilderotter: "The idea was that if an activist was writing a letter to HPE demanding incremental shareholder value, what would it say?"
4. Once the CEO and the board set a long-term strategy for the company, the directors should help management communicate that vision to investors. This does not mean explaining operations, but rather conveying a strong story about the company's strategy and its ESG principles.

Advice from Maggie Wilderotter to CEOs

Things are moving a lot faster today in corporate America, and there's a lot more disruption. Much of this is being driven by digital transformation. As a result, shareholders want results and value creation faster. CEOs of public companies are under intense pressure, and when activists show up it is distracting and time-consuming. Boards need to work with their CEOs to be proactive in creating meaningful shareholder value through the strategic choices they make.

We live in an era where we should know what activists would bring up about the business, and we should be proactive about discussing those issues. I feel all board members have a responsibility to be as knowledgeable as possible about the business so they can do the right thing for shareholders. At HPE the directors worked closely with Meg Whitman and her executive team to formulate a long-term strategy. The board composed a letter as if written by an activist, suggesting which businesses to sell and which ones to keep and build. We were able to do this because many of us had deep technology backgrounds—we knew the competitive field. It's a good way for people to take their director hats off and put on their outside shareholder hat and to come at the problem from a different perspective. If a board doesn't have the right expertise, it can always hire an outside consulting company to help them through the exercise.

The key to making these "activist letter" exercises work is for the leadership to be open to the board's input and suggestions. At the same time, the board needs to show a lot of respect for the leadership because they know what they are doing in their industry. It's all about discussion and dialogue, and the directors being able to engage with the leadership on what they're doing, what the customers are telling us, what the numbers are telling us, and what they are worried about. As directors, we also need to encourage management to make a major pivot or shift if we think that's what's needed.

I probably spend more time getting involved than other directors. My type of behavior is getting more common, but I'm still an outlier. I feel it's a responsibility that all board members step up and help CEOs do the right thing for the long-term health of the business, the employees, and the shareholders.

Part Two
Why Long-Term Thinking Is Your Best Short-Term Strategy

Chapter 7

Going Long Works

Going long works. Now is the time to step up and make it happen.

A s we've seen from the CEO accounts in this book, going long is not easy, but it can be done. CEOs who figure out how to manage their organizations for the long term will be rewarded for their efforts. Solid long-term strategies executed well can help your business leapfrog the competition. They can also create jobs, build public trust, improve the environment, and, in the end, richly reward shareholders.

It bears repeating that there are many ways for CEOs to go long. Different industries have different time horizons. A high-tech firm might have a two-year cycle and a pharmaceutical company a 10-year cycle. But as Jeff Bezos reminds us, you have to think longer term than your competitor. If everyone else is planning three years out, you can gain a great advantage by thinking seven years out. It will be lonely out there, but thinking this way will allow you to stay one step ahead of the competition.

Different CEOs also have their own distinct value systems and approaches for going long. Some try to build sustainable organizations that embrace such ESG issues as alleviating global poverty, improving public health, or reducing their company's carbon footprint to zero. Others focus on maximizing shareholder returns—not for this quarter or next but years or even decades from now. By thinking in these terms, CEOs often end up in the same place as those leaders who embrace ESG issues: they create jobs, reduce their impact on the environment (which in most cases saves money), and generate wealth for shareholders.

Despite these different approaches, we have found that there are four broad, basic principles that any CEO who wishes to adopt a long game can follow:

1. Create a purpose for your organization that is greater than just profits.
2. Translate that purpose into a long-term business strategy and then get strong buy-in from your board and your investors.
3. Formulate metrics beyond EPS and near-term financial performance that help directors and investors understand whether the business is making progress on its long-term goals.
4. Finally, foster a culture that always focuses on long-term, profitable growth to make sure that your long-term strategy is well executed.

Develop a Purpose Greater Than Profits

Long-term financial goals and metrics are necessary but not sufficient for success. CEOs must find a purpose that motivates employees. It is important for a company's rank and file to feel like their jobs have meaning, that they are able to contribute to the company's success, and that they are part of something bigger than themselves. It is the job of top management to communicate that. Any CEO seeking to create a purpose-led organization must find ways to win over both internal and external constituencies. This requires a lot more than making pronouncements about having a "purpose." It means making sure your employees and suppliers not only understand the purpose of the company but also act in ways that support that purpose.

As we saw in chapter 3, Unilever's Paul Polman decided to seek a purpose greater than profits—the alleviation of poverty and a zero carbon footprint. To do so, he created a business model that takes other constituencies into account. This means injecting ESG issues directly into the company's DNA. It means running a business profitably but also making sure employees, customers, suppliers, and the community at large benefit from the corporation's activities. The purpose must be integrated into the organization's day-to-day operations, with hard-headed metrics to track progress. This formula works. Unilever's stock over Polman's tenure has handily outperformed that of its peers.

But this is not the only way to manage with a long-term purpose. For some CEOs, ESG is not an end unto itself but rather a healthy by-product of their company's long-term strategy and investment decisions. As we sketched out in chapter 2, when CVS Health CEO Larry Merlo took a huge gamble by dropping cigarette sales—a move that cost the retailer $2 billion in short-term annual revenues—he sent a clear and convincing message to his employees, customers, and investors that the company was dead serious about becoming a leading healthcare company by helping people lead healthier lifestyles. The move helped CVS sign up more hospitals, health plans, and other healthcare customers, driving growth in that segment of its business.

In either case, focusing on a broader target than profits can energize employees, help shape short-term decisions, and boost the bottom line.

Pound Home Your Strategy to Investors

CEOs who take the long road often come under pressure from investors who want high returns today, not tomorrow. When capital is used to fund an ambitious R&D program, build talent, or develop a new marketing campaign, hedge funds and other activist investors might circle, demanding the money be used instead to buy back stock or boost dividends. Any CEO who wants to avoid becoming a target must think like an activist and cut costs or sell off businesses before the activists do it for them. This means creating a long-term strategy that promises to pay off far more than simply cutting costs and returning the cash to shareholders.

As we learned from HPE director Maggie Wilderotter in chapter 6, CEOs who want to go long should seek out the wisdom and backing of board members who deeply understand the company's strategy, can engage in give-and-take with the executive team, spend sufficient time to solve difficult problems together, and show mutual respect for one another. To help crystalize a new long-term strategy for HPE, the board composed a letter to management as if an activist had written it.

To keep activists away, CEOs need to formulate a clear and compelling business case that the board and their long-term investors can back with enthusiasm. When doing this they need to remember that not all investors are alike. Short-term traders won't have your back but plenty of long-term investors will if you can reach out and persuade them to take the journey with you. The growing influence of index funds—which now represent a large and growing share of the US equity market and are by definition long-term investors—means that there are influential players in the market who want CEOs to manage for the long term, as do many of the pension funds and university endowments that entrust their money to such funds. The challenge is to clearly articulate your strategy, explain it clearly and consistently to board members and long-term investors, listen to their advice and always keep them in the loop.

Measure Long-Term Success

Any CEO who wants to achieve healthy long-term growth must have a clear way to measure progress. Otherwise it's easy to let the company's long-term vision fall to the wayside, as pressing daily issues take everyone's time and attention. Going long at times requires huge capital investments—it can be incredibly expensive—and investors need to be reassured that the plan is working. As we learned in chapter 4, Verizon CEO Ivan Seidenberg spent $150 billion on building his wireless and broadband networks. He told his investors that his long-term goal was to create the best products and services in the telecommunications industry. He then picked a clear, easy-to-understand metric as a defining element of long-term growth. Seidenberg chose market share growth—because it provided strong evidence that consumers wanted his products—to show his investors that his long-term strategy was on track, quarter after quarter, year after year. Of course, every market is different. In some industries, for example, you can pick up market share by cutting prices, but that might not do you any good in the long run. Pick the metric that works best for your market.

Ford's Alan Mulally, as we explained in chapter 1, used a different long-term metric. He implemented what he calls PGA, or "profitable growth for all," to get everyone focused on the long-term fundamentals. Yet managing long isn't just about profit sheet metrics. It makes sense to also track metrics that cover both performance and health, measurements that show the progress you are making in building a stronger company. These include, but are not limited to, levels of customer satisfaction, employee engagement, and degree of growth from new products or whatever it is that is tailored to your strategy.

Create a Culture Focused on the Long Run

When going long, CEOs need to create a culture that shares a clear vision of the future. They need to develop a team that's open enough and trusting enough to do what it takes to build products and services people want and improve productivity every year. Getting people to focus on the long term helps everyone make the right decisions for the short term. That means fostering a culture that is brutally honest about what's working and not working within the organization. Companies that let problems fester end up paying the price in the long term. Getting people to be honest with each other means helping them listen to and respect each other's opinions. Once you get a team working together, they are much better able to solve problems no matter what happens, be it a financial crisis, safety issues, or new competitors.

As we explored in chapter 5, 3M's Sir George Buckley created a culture where people felt they were not only supported by the executive team but also felt safe to take risks and fail. He did this by green-lighting R&D programs that his scientists and engineers had thought to be promising but had sat on the shelf during the previous regime, encouraging them to take big risks, and, notably, not punishing them for failure. Buckley showed his employees that he had a plausible and defensible dream for 3M's future and followed through with actions that showed them he believed in the dream. Over his tenure Buckley grew the share of new products that had been launched in the previous five years from 8% of sales to 34% of sales.

Successful CEOs don't go long for the sake of going long. It's what a company gets from acting long term that matters. Long-term companies can outstrip competitors and position themselves for a bright future 5, 10, or even 15 years out. And as we've seen from the CEOs in this book who had the courage to think long, they created jobs, pleased customers, made their communities richer, and, of course, made their shareholders richer.

What these CEOs did wasn't easy. Next, we will hear from some of the most powerful investors in the world and how they are planning to help CEOs make long-term management the rule, rather than the exception.

Chapter 8

Helping CEOs to Think Long

New ideas about executive pay, the role of index funds, and how the stock market works could trigger a renaissance in long-term management.

You hear of CEOs getting calls from a junior analyst asking what last week's inventory turns were. It was all focused on the short run.
—William McNabb, chairman of Vanguard

To encourage CEOs to go long, our leadership models need to change. If CEOs are to succeed, they need to operate in an ecosystem that encourages long-term management. So how can we create a world where going long is the norm? For a start, institutional investors must work more closely with boards and CEOs to give their support and to make sure companies stay on a long track. For example, as we've mentioned, big asset managers such as BlackRock, Vanguard, and State Street, which through their index funds represent an increasingly large share of the US equity markets, are starting to get more actively engaged in advising boards on what they think will create long-term value. In some instances they can provide support for CEOs who wish to go long, a move that can cost in the short term but ultimately pays off.

Another idea that's gaining currency in some investing circles is to make a portion of CEO restricted stock grants vest five years or more *after* the executive leaves the company, to encourage long-term thinking in the C-suite. Even stock exchanges are ripe for change. A group of Silicon Valley titans believes that stock markets could be designed to reward long-term investing. They are planning to launch the Long-Term Stock Exchange, a trading platform meant to reward investors who give CEOs enough time to execute their complex long-term strategies.

Create Really Long-Term Stock Incentives

There is a growing perception among some investors and boards that executive compensation needs to encourage more long-term thinking. Vanguard chairman William McNabb, whose company manages $5 trillion in assets, is proposing to take a portion of a CEO's restricted stock grants and vest it 5 to 10 years *after* the executive leaves the business. He explains: "The median tenure of a CEO is six years, and there is no way you can judge how well or poorly someone has done in that time frame. Someone who only lasts a short time in the job can make a lot of decisions that help them in the short run but not in the long run. I think finding a way to keep a linkage there might help change behavior."[66]

Typically, a CEO's restricted stock grants vest after three years. Some companies like ExxonMobil encourage long-term thinking by vesting one-half of restricted stock grants in 5 years and the other half in 10 years.[67] In the absence of this long-term incentive, a CEO of ExxonMobil might be tempted to cut back on exploration, which would bump up short-term earnings and make the CEO look like a hero to investors—for a while. Ultimately the CEO's successor would bear the brunt of that short-term move, which would show up as diminishing oil and gas reserves. Says McNabb: "We can all think of companies where the CEO rode the PE [price-earnings] multiple expansion and the successor was stuck with an incredibly high valuation which is bound to come back to earth. In those cases, there's no way they're going to look good from a long-term shareholder return standpoint."

Critics of the plan say that delaying executive pay that far out would only put greater burdens on CEOs and create yet another reason for companies not to go public. "The fundamental problem that we have," argues BlackRock CEO Larry Fink, "is that we're attacking more public CEOs. I think one of the greatest risks we have is that fewer and fewer companies are going public. It's become harder and harder." (For less radical ways to encourage long-term thinking through compensation, see the "Paying for Long-Term Results" sidebar.)

Paying for Long-Term Results

Corporations that want to manage for the long run need executive compensation packages that support that behavior. Compensation systems are complicated, and different industries have different needs. One system we like was created by ITT CEO Denise Ramos. Here's how it works.

After taking on the top job at ITT in 2011, Ramos saw that this manufacturer of brake pads, aerospace parts, oil and gas pumps, and other precision parts needed more long-term focus. After all, the company is grounded and rooted in long-term partnerships. For example, the high-tech brake pads that ITT makes for the auto industry represent much more than one-off sales. They require cementing a long-term relationship with the customer that includes replacement parts and service. If a customer isn't happy with their supplier, the fallout can be devastating. That's because each new car model is on the market for a long stretch before being replaced with the next generation. "If you don't get to sell to those auto platforms, you'll be closed out of the market for 7 to 8 years," says Ramos.[68]

Few things can hurt a long-term relationship with a customer more than short-term thinking. Cutting corners, pulling back on service, and other moves that can boost quarterly earnings can often cause rifts in a relationship. How to avoid that fate? ITT executives earn part of their bonus based on four metrics: revenue, margins, cash flow, and EPS—nothing terribly new about that. But here is where its bonus system gets interesting: Ramos evaluates her direct reports based on the quality of their long-term thinking. Ten percent of the bonus plan rewards how executives perform from a strategic perspective. She explains: "I evaluate my team based on whether they are doing things that are

(continued)

more long term than short term, and whether they are driving key strategic initiatives that you wouldn't ordinarily see in the annual numbers."

Ramos says she rewards executives who advance the company's strategy to shift into new markets and who turn those strategic ideas into tangible actions. Anytime the company decides it wants to expand through either acquisitions or new products, a strategic review is done of the market and the opportunity. When contemplating an expansion into the railway industry, for example, the company's CFO, who also leads the strategy function, was heavily involved in determining where product expansion might make sense, and thinking about linkages across the various parts of the business. His broader view of the organization was critical when collaborating with the chief operating officer and business leaders to determine what actions made the most sense and when to execute. His work helped create an action plan and vision not just for the short term but also for the long term, ensuring that ITT's main business remains healthy and competitive for years to come.

"What our chief financial officer did had no impact in terms of our metrics for comp that year," explains Ramos, "but it was something very valuable to the long-term success of our business so he got a strong score on the long-term strategic component of his annual incentive plan."

Ramos also uses return on invested capital as another long-term lever. She wants her executives to be accountable and rewarded for investment decisions that may take years before they realize the benefits. Large investments such as acquisitions or building manufacturing facilities have a short-term impact on cash expenditures but with the expectation of higher profits in the future. ITT, for instance, has been investing to expand its brake pad business, but the company's annual performance metrics didn't reflect the short-term work executives were doing on that project. To address this dilemma, Ramos now measures how her executives manage the cash and construction schedules over the short term, which gets reflected in their annual bonuses. Over the long term the executives will be rewarded for achieving return on invested capital targets if they are deploying capital efficiently and on time. Says Ramos, "It is a reflection that these auto part factories will eventually produce great long-term results for the company."

Work More Closely with Investors

What makes McNabb and others optimistic about making our markets more long-term oriented is that investors like Vanguard and BlackRock are taking a more active role in how corporations are governed. These companies largely manage index funds, which by definition have to hold onto every stock in their portfolio—no matter what. Because they have to hold every stock in their sector basically forever, they are concerned about good performance for their investors not just this quarter or the next, but also 5, 10, or even 20 years out.

Index funds have been gaining influence in the stock market. According to BlackRock, they now hold 12% of all US equities, up from less than 1% thirty years ago, and that number is growing rapidly. Passive investors have also been ramping up the number of employees who engage with directors on governance issues. BlackRock now has about 30 people in its investment stewardship function, and CEO Larry Fink says that number will double over the next three years as part of a multiyear plan to expand its efforts. Of course, this isn't a sufficient number of bodies to cover the vast array of governance issues that arise each year at America's roughly 15,000 shareholder meetings, but it does allow these funds, which have enormous voting power, to at least target the most egregious cases of subpar performance.

By contrast, actively managed funds, which still represent the lion's share of the market, don't have much incentive to encourage CEOs to manage for the long run. The turnover in the stock portfolio of a traditional, actively managed mutual fund is 90% annually on average, which means the fund holds each stock for only about a year. That's a high level of turnover. If you include hedge funds, the holding period is even shorter. Says McNabb: "You hear of CEOs getting calls from a junior analyst asking what last week's inventory turns were. It was all focused on the short run. A CEO is never going to get a call from Vanguard asking what the inventory turns were last week. It is just not relevant to us."

What is relevant to Vanguard and other big long-term investors is good corporate governance that leads, they believe, to stronger long-term financial results. Vanguard, for instance, argues that to achieve strong stock performance decade after decade, boards should have a good set of governance rules in place—rules that should include, among other things, performance-based pay, accountability for CEO succession, and a rigorous capital allocation and risk assessment process. "We'd like to see really good governance rules in place that people are living by," says McNabb. "When we don't see that we will be more willing to raise our hands and say, 'There's something amiss here and you better address it.' We hope our advocacy for good governance will create a floor of good behavior that lifts the market over the long term."

BlackRock, State Street, and Vanguard have already had some success in engaging corporate boards on governance issues. Vanguard's investment stewardship officer Glenn Booraem says that his firm now actively engages with directors of the companies they invest in and so far have found them to be responsive to its ideas about better governance. "We're not going to be coming in with 500-page decks like the activists with a new business plan for the company," says Booraem, "but our role is evolving to one of fairly consistent engagement with boards on governance topics."[69] In 2017 Vanguard did 950 engagements with companies, and about a third of those involved independent directors; five years ago that number was almost zero.

As an example, Booraem recalls how Vanguard engaged with a company's directors on compensation. The board had brought in a new CEO and had granted the executive hundreds of millions in equity that would just vest with the passage of time. There was no linkage to long-term performance. "It raised a red flag for us," says Booraem, "and we engaged with the comp committee of the board over a multiyear period." Eventually the board reopened the CEO contract and took a portion of the equity compensation and tied it to relative performance against the S&P 500.

What leverage do index funds like Vanguard really have over boards? After all, they can't dump a company's shares. The proxy vote is what gives them some clout. At one point Vanguard was struggling to get the attention of the board of a real estate investment trust (REIT) that was, says Booraem, "about as poorly governed as it could be, and violated about every good governance principle we had. When we tried to engage they told us to go pound sand."

Eventually an activist got involved who thought that while the REIT had great assets, those assets were being undermanaged. The activist approached Vanguard and said he was thinking about taking a run at the REIT and asked if the firm would back him. Vanguard said yes. Booraem recalls that on the day of the proxy contest, with just 30 minutes to go until the vote, he got a call from a board member of the REIT who said he couldn't believe Vanguard was going to vote against them.

"I can't believe we're having this conversation with 30 minutes to go before the vote closes," Booraem replied. "We've been trying to talk to you for 18 months."

"But you're a passive investor," the director said.

"We're a passive investor, not a passive owner," Booraem answered. "You guys have violated every governing principle and, by the way, you are the worst-performing stock in one of our index funds. And bad governance has a lot to do about it."

The activist and Vanguard won the proxy vote and made the necessary changes to help get the company back on track.

The lesson here is that any board and executive team wanting good relations with their investors should communicate with them before a crisis emerges; they should engage proactively, not reactively. Directors and CEOs need to initiate conversations with their investors early on that explain their long-term thinking, where they stand on particular issues of governance, and how they are moving to correct any shortcomings. Otherwise, directors who don't listen to their investors might find themselves on the wrong side of a proxy fight.

Change the Rules to Reward Long-Term Investors

CEOs who manage for the short term use the stock market as their report card. When their stock goes up, so does their bonus—and their mood. When it starts to falter, they scramble to cut costs and heads to make their quarterly numbers. This, of course, is not good for the long-term health of the company or its investors, employees, and the communities it serves. But what if CEOs had investors who got rewarded for backing their long-term strategies?

A group of Silicon Valley titans is addressing this issue but is taking a different tack. They believe that stock market indexes could be designed to reward long-term investing. As of the writing of this book, they plan to launch the Long-Term Stock Exchange (LTSE), a trading platform meant to turn corporate governance on its head. The LTSE is the creation of venture capitalist Marc Andreessen of Andreessen Horowitz, an early investor in Facebook; Reid Hoffman, the founder of LinkedIn; and Eric Ries, an author and start-up expert who serves as the exchange's CEO.[70] The group says it has raised $19 million from around 70 investors. It is aiming to get regulatory approval to start operating in 2018.[71]

Ries first floated the notion for his exchange in his 2011 book *The Lean Startup*. The idea was to get investors focused not on short-term financial results but on long-term strategies. The voting power of shares traded on the LTSE increases the longer investors own them and, after a decade, are capped at 10 times more votes per share than regular common stock. If the shares are sold, they would be reset to one vote per share for the new owner.

Companies listed on the exchange have to agree to certain principles of corporate governance, such as a ban on tying executive pay to the company's short-term financial performance. Executive bonuses can't be tied to financial-performance targets of periods of less than one year. Restricted stock grants can't fully vest for at least five years. Companies on the LTSE still publish quarterly results (which is a requirement of the Securities and Exchange Commission), but they can't give quarterly earnings guidance.

Skeptics wonder whether the LTSE is just another way for tech founders and elite Silicon Valley investors to maintain control of their start-ups at the expense of other shareholders. There's also the danger that such a system could lead to entrenched managements. The founders of the LTSE disagree, however, saying that disgruntled share-holders would still have a say through proxy votes, but that the power would rest in long-term holders rather than quick-hit activists.

Many of the ideas examined in this chapter aimed at focusing CEOs on the long term have merit, but it is not yet clear which are winners and which are losers. Strong political and financial interests could easily stand in the way of implementing, or at least delay implementation of, many of these ideas. The point is that change is coming. A growing movement to make the American economy more long-term oriented is on the rise, and we believe it's here to stay. In the next chapter we will explore the societal pressures driving this movement.

Chapter 9

Mastering Tomorrow

Going forward, CEOs must find a balance between rewarding share-holders and serving their employees, consumers, and society.

CEOs need to look at how the world is changing and ask them-selves how their company fits into these huge societal changes that are impacting all of us.

—Larry Fink, CEO of BlackRock

Shannon Mulcahy is a steel worker from Indianapolis. As portrayed in a moving *New York Times* profile in the fall of 2017, this single mother of two, after 18 years of working as a skilled technician running a machine that makes forged roller bearings, learned that her company, Rexnord, was moving the factory to Monterrey, Mexico, and that, as a result, she was out of a high-paying job.

Todd Adams, the CEO of Rexnord, had to make a tough decision. Workers like Mulcahy earned an average of $25 an hour. In Mexico, by contrast, he would have to pay skilled workers only $6 an hour. Competition from cheap labor in Asia was making some of Rexnord's made-in-America products uncompetitive. The company had tried to automate parts of the plant, but even so, moving the roller bearing facility to Mexico would shrink annual costs by $30 million.

While workers like Shannon were losing their jobs, Adams was earning roughly $40 million over six years, in part for cutting costs at Rexnord. There is little, if any, indication that he or his successors will do their jobs any differently going forward. Unfortunately, this is what the future holds for blue-collar workers like Mulcahy and many of the 67% of adults in this country who do not have a four-year college degree.

The factory's shuttering became part of the national debate. "Rexnord of Indianapolis is moving to Mexico and rather viciously firing all of its 300 workers," tweeted the then president-elect Donald Trump in December 2016. "No more!"[72]

The president's tweet made no difference to the fate of the factory, but it did raise the question of the proper role for a corporation in the twenty-first century. Should it be to maximize shareholder value or to balance those interests against those of employees, customers, the government, and local communities?

We'd argue these choices do not have to be mutually exclusive. The best way to maximize shareholder return over the long term is to run a corporation in a way that will generate "profitable growth for all," as Ford's Alan Mulally says earlier in this book. In this context, "all" means not just shareholders but also employees, suppliers, customers, and the communities in which they all live.

Yes, the end goal is to maximize shareholder returns, but what exactly does that mean in today's world? We believe that managing for the long term is all about investing in R&D and workforce training, and finding environmentally and socially sustainable ways to operate. This is the way to create more good American jobs, and it's also the best way to maximize shareholder return decade after decade.

Why now? Part of the Trump movement in the 2016 elections was built on the notion that both the government and corporate America have been letting the middle class down. This was not a figment of Donald Trump's imagination. According to the Pew Research Center, 37% of Americans now view American corporations unfavorably, up from 25% in 2001. At the same time, 60% of Americans look favorably on labor unions.[73]

One of the main reasons many Americans distrust corporations stems from a fear that they will take away their jobs. "The fundamental problem we have now," says BlackRock's Fink, "is that capital is taking the place of human beings in the name of efficiencies. Think about the U.S. We have 4% unemployment, a growing economy and things feel really good. Yet there's this gigantic anger about the future. Capital is winning out and the owner of capital wins when machines replace humans."

Consider for a moment the potential disruption that self-driving vehicles could cause. Tesla's Elon Musk announced in late 2017 that he would build a self-driving electric truck.[74] That threatens the jobs of America's 3.5 million truck drivers.[75] Around the same time, Volvo announced it would deliver 24,000 self-driving taxis to Uber starting in 2019.[76] What will happen to Uber's estimated 7 million drivers worldwide?[77]

A study by the McKinsey Global Institute found that a billion workers around the world could be displaced by automation by 2030.[78] In the United States, the displacement could involve up to one-third of the workforce. The jobs most likely to disappear are those that involve collecting and processing data (like accounting, mortgage origination, and paralegal work) or jobs that involve manual labor in predictable environments (like operating machinery or making fast food).

Another factor CEOs need to take into account is the rising activism of millennials. Those born between 1982 and 2000, according to the US Census Bureau,[79] have now surpassed baby boomers as the nation's largest living generation. While this cohort, some 83.1 million strong, is made up of individuals with many diverse views, one thing you can say is that many of them take the environment and social issues very seriously. According to a 2011 study by ad agency network TBWA/Worldwide and TakePart, the digital division of Participant Media, 7 in 10 young adults consider themselves social activists. More tellingly, some 80% said they would be more likely to buy products and services from companies that support their causes.[80]

Millennials apply these same attitudes to the investing world. According to the 2017 Wealth and Worth report, released by US Trust

Figure 2. Technology Threatens a Billion Jobs

Using currently demonstrated technologies, the number of tasks that can be automated would affect $14 trillion in wages and a billion jobs by 2030

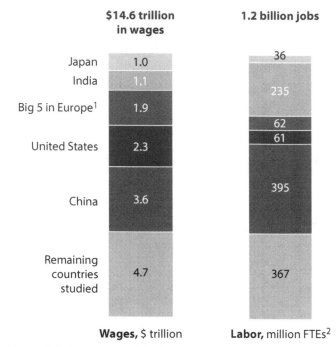

$14.6 trillion in wages | 1.2 billion jobs

Wages, $ trillion   Labor, million FTEs[2]

[1]France, Germany, Italy, Spain, and United Kingdom.
[2]FTEs = full-time equivalents.

Source: McKinsey Global Institute, A Future That Works: Automation, Employment, and Productivity, January 2017.

(Bank of America's private wealth management arm), 76% of millennials said they consider their investment decisions to be a way to express their social, political, and environmental values, and 88% said that a company's impact in these areas is an important consideration when they make investment decisions.[81]

So the business environment has changed, and CEOs need to respond, but they will be hard put to do it without the backing of their investors.

Investors Who Drive Change

For all the Sturm und Drang caused by activists and hedge funds, some 75% of the world's stock market capitalization is held by long-term institutions such as pension funds and university endowments. For the most part, they, and not the activists, should be driving the business world.[82] Over the past decade we've seen a sea change in the way these institutions think about investing. Many of them now believe that a corporation's responsibility is broader than maximizing shareholder return.

As part of this trend, a growing number of big institutional investors, including pension funds and university endowments, are putting pressure on companies to adopt more rigorous ESG standards. Nonprofits such as Ceres, a network of investors that encourages companies to engage in climate change solutions; the Sustainability Accounting Standards Board, which asks companies to adopt transparent reporting on ESG issues; and the Investor Stewardship Group, which encourages strong corporate governance principles, have as members pension funds and university endowments that want to make capitalism more sustainable and more inclusive. One of the biggest of such organizations is called Principles for Responsible Investing (PRI), which was launched in 2006. Globally, some 1,900 investors who cumulatively manage roughly $70 trillion in assets have joined this nonprofit.[83] Says Abe Friedman, the founder and CEO of CamberView Partners, an advisor on corporate governance, investor engagement, and activism that counts over 170 companies, including nearly 50 Fortune 100 companies, as clients: "CEOs have never been under more pressure to show that they care about sustainability and society. It's become really critical."[84]

Investors that become PRI members agree to follow six broad principles that are meant to foster a sustainable global financial system. They include incorporating ESG issues into investment analysis and decision-making processes, becoming active owners, and seeking appropriate disclosure on ESG issues by the entities in which they invest. In practice this means that the big institutional investors that

Figure 3. Investors Push CEOs to Be More Socially Aware

Some 1,900 institutional investors who control $70 trillion in assets now support PRI's standards for sustainable investment.

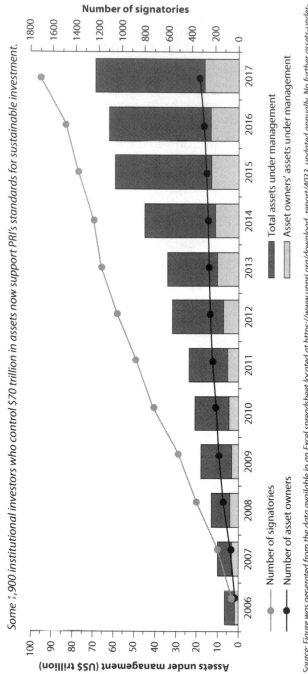

Number of signatories

Assets under management (US$ trillion)

— Number of signatories
— Number of asset owners

Total assets under management
Asset owners' assets under management

Source: Figure was generated from the data available in an Excel spreadsheet located at https://www.unpri.org/download_report/4033, updated annually. No further assets-under-management breakdowns by asset class, country, region, or signatory category are available.

belong to PRI, like Calpers, Calsters, and the Harvard University Endowment, are asking BlackRock, Vanguard, State Street, and other asset managers to invest the money they give them in companies that follow ESG practices.

The asset managers are happy to do this because they believe it gives them a competitive advantage. "There are only three ways an index fund can differentiate itself: on price, on service, and by saying I'm a better steward of your assets," says CamberView's Friedman. "There's not much room left to compete on the first two these days, so it's become all about good stewardship."

Consider that in the spring of 2017 both BlackRock and Vanguard voted in favor of a shareholder proposal sponsored by the New York State Pension Fund and the Church of England investment fund that would force ExxonMobil to report the impact on its oil and gas businesses of global measures aimed at limiting climate change to 2 degrees centigrade. BlackRock and Vanguard are ExxonMobil's biggest shareholders. The climate change proposal garnered 62.3% of the vote.[85]

BlackRock and the other asset managers supported the shareholder proposal because they are trying to ensure both strong long-term gains for their shareholders and a livable planet. Says BlackRock's Fink: "CEOs need to look at how the world is changing and ask themselves how their company fits into these huge societal changes that are impacting all of us. Socially, people believe we have to hear from energy companies on what a carbon-free world would look like and what climate change will do to their businesses and how they are going to adapt."

If we want to preserve and strengthen capitalism—which until now has been the greatest creator of wealth in history—corporations need to operate in ways that restore trust in the system. For some CEOs, like Unilever's Paul Polman, this means injecting ESG issues directly into the company's DNA. As Polman has said, he's out to better the lives of a billion of the world's disadvantaged by selling food, soap, and other packaged goods that are affordable and healthful in the developing world.

But this is not the only way to manage for the long term and please big investors. For some CEOs, ESG is not an end unto itself but rather a healthy by-product of their company's long-term strategy and investment decisions. When Ivan Seidenberg invested $150 billion to build out Verizon's wireless and broadband businesses he was thinking about creating the best communications system in America. In the process he ended up creating tens of thousands of new, high-paying jobs—a boon for American society. Says CamberView's Friedman: "I think companies are finding ways to deal with this issue in a way that drives their business forward. There is a false dichotomy out there that says you can either focus on social issues or on the bottom-line. Investors want companies to create value for the long term. Most companies can find an intersection between driving value and demonstrating the societal benefits of that value creation."

Whether or not a CEO puts ESG issues front and center, one thing that distinguishes a long-term strategy from a short-term one is whether a leader considers the consequences for all of the company's constituencies. When Alan Mulally was turning around Ford, his mantra was PGA—"profitable growth for all." What that meant in practice was that whenever he and his executive team were making long-term decisions they asked themselves whether it would be good not only for shareholders but also for employees, suppliers, customers, and the community. As an example, Mulally wanted Ford to build the best vehicles ever made. In one sense that meant making the most fuel-efficient cars possible, which would help reduce pollution.

It's easy for CEOs to say that it's not their job to worry about the rest of the country. To keep America strong, however, we need a stable citizenry working good-paying jobs so they can support a family and a community. If we stay on the track we're on, that's not going to happen. If we want to strengthen capitalism, we need to change how our corporations operate. The examples in this book of CEOs going long need to be replicated throughout the system to save the benefits of capitalism while helping to prevent its abuses.

The "Go Long" CEOs profiled in this book have shown that it is possible to manage for the long term and maximize returns to their shareholders while creating good jobs and helping society.

So why not go long? Time is running short.

Notes

1 Focusing Capital on the Long Term, *A Roadmap for Focusing Capital on the Long Term*, March 2015, https://www.fcltglobal.org/docs/default-source/default-document-library/a-roadmap-for-fclt.pdf?sfvrsn=0.

2 New York Stock Exchange, "Annual Reported Volume, Turnover Rate, Reported Trades (mils. of shares)," 2004, http://www.nyxdata.com/nysedata/asp/factbook/viewer_edition.asp?mode=table&key=2206&category=4.

3 Ronald Orol, "5 Things We Learned about Activist Investing in 2017," TheStreet, December 30, 2017, https://www.thestreet.com/story/14430880/1/five-things-we-learned-about-activist-investing-in-2017.html.

4 Chris Plath, "Activists Set for Another Record Year, but Fervor Is Cooling," *Shareholder Activism 2015*, November 10, 2015, p. 2, https://www.thecorporatecounsel.net/nonmember/docs/2016_Activism.pdf.

5 Michael Ide, "Activist Funds: From Zero to $100B Plus AUM in 20 Years," Value Walk, February 26, 2015, http://www.valuewalk.com/2015/02/activist-funds-aima/.

6 Obi Ezekoye, Tim Koller, and Ankit Mittal, "How Share Repurchases Boost Earnings without Improving Returns," McKinsey & Company, April 2016.

7 Cited in Joe Ciolli, "America's Biggest Companies Are Investing More in Themselves—and It's Causing a Huge Shift in the Stock Market," Business Insider, October 30, 2017, http://www.businessinsider.com/stock-market-news-capex-spending-causing-huge-shift-2017-10.

8 Dominic Barton, James Manyika, Tim Koller, Robert Palter, Jonathan Godsall, and Josh Zoffer, "Where Companies with a Long-Term View Outperform Their Peers," McKinsey Global Institute, February 2017, https://www.mckinsey.com/global-themes/long-term-capitalism/where-companies-with-a-long-term-view-outperform-their-peers.

9 Ibid.

10 Rebecca Darr and Tim Koller, "How to Build an Alliance against Corporate Short-Termism," McKinsey & Company, January 2017.

11 Peter Krass, *The Book of Management Wisdom: Classic Writings by Legendary Managers* (New York: John Wiley & Sons, 2000), p. 358.

12 Dave Namo, "Socialism's Rising Popularity Threatens America's Future," *National Review*, March 18, 2017.

13 Harvard Institute of Politics, "Clinton in Commanding Lead over Trump among Young Voters, Harvard Youth Poll Finds," Harvard University IOP at The Kennedy School, April 25, 2016, http://iop.harvard.edu/youth-poll/past/harvard-iop-spring-2016-poll.

14 Martin Lipton, "Corporate Governance—the New Paradigm," Harvard Law School Forum on Corporate Governance and Financial Regulation, September 1, 2017, https://corpgov.law.harvard.edu/2017/09/01/corporate-governance-the-new-paradigm-2/.

15 Ed Breen, interview by the authors, CEO Academy Conference, 2016.

16 Neal E. Boudette, Joann S. Lublin, and Christina Rogers, "Mulally's Legacy: Setting Ford on a Stronger Course," *Wall Street Journal*, April 21, 2014, https://www.wsj.com/articles/fords-operating-chief-to-become-ceo-this-year-sources-1398104995.

17 Unless otherwise noted, all Alan Mulally quotations in this chapter are from interviews by the authors.

18 Card reprinted with permission from Alan Mulally.

19 Bryce G. Hoffman, *American Icon: Alan Mulally and the Fight to Save Ford Motor Company* (New York: Crown Business, 2012), p. 31.

20 Mike Isaac, "Uber Founder Travis Kalanick Resigns as C.E.O.," *New York Times*, June 21, 2017, https://www.nytimes.com/2017/06/21/technology/uber-ceo-travis-kalanick.html?_r=0.

21 Hoffman, *American Icon*, p. 31.

22 Michael Useem, *Leading Up: How to Lead Your Boss So You Both Win* (New York: Crown Business/Random House, 2001).

23 Markus MacGill, "Half of All American Adults Have a Chronic Disease—CDC," Medical News Today, July 2, 2014, https://www.medicalnewstoday.com/articles/279084.php.

24 Aurel O. Iuga and Maura J. McGuire, "Adherence and Health Care Costs," Dove Press, February 20, 2014, https://www.ncbi.nlm.nih.gov/pmc/articles/PMC3934668/.

25 Unless otherwise noted, all Larry Merlo quotations in this chapter are from interviews by the authors.

26 Leah McGrath Goodman, "Why CVS Went Cold Turkey," *Newsweek*, February 6, 2014, http://www.newsweek.com/cvs-stubs-out-cigarettes-sell-more-drugs-228151.

27 Jayne O'Donnell and Laura Ungar, "CVS Stops Selling Tobacco, Offers Quit-Smoking Programs," *USA Today*, September 3, 2014, https://www.usatoday.com/story/news/nation/2014/09/03/cvs-steps-selling-tobacco-changes-name/14967821/.

28 Ronnie Cohen, "When CVS Stopped Selling Cigarettes, Some Customers Quit Smoking," Reuters, March 20, 2017, https://www.reuters.com/article/us-health-pharmacies-cigarettes/when-cvs-stopped-selling-cigarettes-some-customers-quit-smoking-idUSKBN16R2HY.

29 O'Donnell and Ungar, "CVS Stops Selling Tobacco, Offers Quit-Smoking Programs."

30 Reed Abelson and Michael J. de la Merced, "CVS to Buy Aetna for $69 Billion in a Deal That May Reshape the Health Industry," *New York Times*, December 3, 2017, https://www.nytimes.com/2017/12/03/business/dealbook/cvs-is-said-to-agree-to-buy-aetna-reshaping-health-care-industry.html.

31 Unless otherwise noted, all Paul Polman quotations in this chapter are from interviews by the authors.

32 Umair Irfan, "Energy Hog Google Just Bought Enough Renewables to Power Its Operations for the Year," Vox, December 6, 2017, https://www.vox.com/energy-and-environment/2017/12/6/16734228/google-renewable-energy-wind-solar-2017.

33 Kaiser Permanente, "About Kaiser Permanente," 2018, https://share.kaiserpermanente.org/about-kaiser-permanente/.

34 National Committee for Quality Insurance, "NCQA Health Insurance Plan Ratings 2016–2017—Summary Report (Private)," June 30, 2016, http://healthinsuranceratings.ncqa.org/2016/default.aspx.

35 Twitter, "Company," 2018, https://about.twitter.com/en_us/company.html.

36 Unilever, "Unilever Puts Vitality at Core of New Mission," 2018, https://www.unilever.com/news/Press-releases/2004/04-02-12-Unilever-puts-vitality-at-core-of-new-mission.html.

37 James Fontanella-Khan and Arash Massoudi, "The $143bn Flop: How Warren Buffett and 3G Lost Unilever," *Financial Times*, February 21, 2017, https://www.ft.com/content/d846766e-f81b-11e6-bd4e-68d53499ed71.

38 Jim Collins and Jerry I. Porras, "Building Your Company's Vision," *Harvard Business Review*, September 1996, https://hbr.org/1996/09/building-your-companys-vision.

39 Wikipedia, s.v. "Port Sunlight," last modified December 20, 2017, https://en.wikipedia.org/wiki/Port_Sunlight.

40 Rick Wartzman, "What Unilever Shares with Google and Apple," *Fortune*, January 7, 2015, http://fortune.com/2015/01/07/what-unilever-shares-with-google-and-apple/.

41 Vivienne Walt, "Unilever CEO Paul Polman's Plan to Save the World," *Fortune*, February 17, 2017, http://fortune.com/2017/02/17/unilever-paul-polman-responsibility-growth/.

42 J.D. Power, "Verizon Wireless Ranks Highest in Wireless Network Quality Performance in All Six Regions; U.S. Cellular Ties for Highest Rank in North Central Region," March 2, 2017, http://www.jdpower.com/press-releases/jd-power-2017-us-wireless-network-quality-performance-study.

43 Verizon, "Verizon Sweeps J.D. Power 2017 U.S. Business Wireline Satisfaction Study," July 25, 2017, http://www.verizon.com/about/our-company/verizon-sweeps-jd-power-2017-us-business-wireline-satisfaction-study.

44   Bob Bryan, "The Biggest Force Powering the Stock Market Is Starting to Disappear, and It Could Be a Huge Problem," Business Insider, March 12, 2016, http://www .businessinsider.com/buybacks-disappearing-could-mean-recession-2016-3.

45   Berkshire Hathaway Inc., "Letter to Shareholders," February 25, 2017, p. 8, http:// www.berkshirehathaway.com/letters/2016ltr.pdf.

46   PWC, "CEO Turnover at a Record High Globally, with More Companies Planning for New Chiefs from outside the Company," April 16, 2016, https://press.pwc.com /News-releases/ceo-turnover-at-a-record-high-globally—with-more-companies -planning-for-new-chiefs-from-outside-the/s/f37f4811 8fca-4b21-ae8b -2e11c3c10561.

47   Unless otherwise noted, all Larry Fink quotations in this book are from interviews by the authors.

48   Nasdaq, "Verizon Communications Inc. Ownership Summary," January 18, 2018, http://www.nasdaq.com/symbol/vz/ownership-summary.

49   Unless otherwise noted, all Ivan Seidenberg quotations in this chapter are from interviews by the authors.

50   Stephanie N. Mehta, "Verizon's Big Bet on Fiber Optics," Fortune, February 22, 2017, http://archive.fortune.com/magazines/fortune/fortune_archive/2007/03/05 /8401289/index.htm.

51   Robin Wigglesworth, "Final Call for the Research Analyst?," Financial Times, February 27, 2017, https://www.ft.com/content/85ee225a-ec4e-11e6-930f -061b01e23655.

52   Unless otherwise noted, all George Buckley quotations in this chapter are from interviews by the authors.

53   Gregory Bresiger, "Investors See Opportunity as Taxi Medallion Prices 'Bottom Out,'" New York Post, October 14, 2017, https://nypost.com/2017/10/14/investors -see-opportunity-as-taxi-medallion-prices-bottom-out/.

54   Innosight, "Corporate Longevity: Turbulence Ahead for Large Organizations," 2016, https://www.innosight.com/insight/creative-destruction/.

55   Ibid.

56   John C. Coffee and Darius Palia, The Wolf at the Door: The Impact of Hedge Fund Activism on Corporate Governance (Delft, The Netherlands: Now Publishers, 2016).

57   Akio Morita, Edwin M. Reingold, and Mitsuko Shimomura, Made in Japan: Akio Morita and Sony (New York: E. P. Dutton, 1986), p. 157.

58   Christine Wang, "Apple's Cash Hoard Swells to Record $256.8 Billion," CNBC, May 2, 2017, https://www.cnbc.com/2017/05/02/apples-cash-hoard-swells-to -record-256-8-billion.html.

59   Andres Cardenal, "Dear Alphabet: Show Me the Money!," Seeking Alpha, December 18, 2017, https://seekingalpha.com/article/4132577-dear-alphabet -show-money.

60 Erin Griffith, "Why Activist Investors Are Targeting the Tech Industry," *Fortune*, July 21, 2015, http://fortune.com/2015/07/21/activist-investors-tech-companies/.

61 Makani, "Team," 2017, https://x.company/makani/team/.

62 Marc Gunther, "3M's Innovation Revival," *Fortune*, September 24, 2010, http://archive.fortune.com/2010/09/23/news/companies/3m_innovation_revival.fortune/index.htm.

63 GradSpeeches, "Carl Icahn Graduation Speech—Video & Transcript," June 14, 2008, http://gradspeeches.com/2008/2008/carl-icahn.

64 Ana Dutra, "A More Effective Board of Directors," *Harvard Business Review*, November 5, 2012, https://hbr.org/2012/11/a-more-effective-board-of-dire.

65 Unless otherwise noted, all Maggie Wilderotter quotations in this chapter are from interviews by the authors.

66 Unless otherwise noted, all William McNabb quotations in this chapter are from interviews by the authors.

67 Joseph E. Bachelder, "Should Executive Pay Be More 'Long-Term'?," Harvard Law School Forum on Corporate Governance and Financial Regulation, April 10, 2017, https://corpgov.law.harvard.edu/2017/04/10/should-executive-pay-be-more-long-term/.

68 Unless otherwise noted, all Denise Ramos quotations in this chapter are from interviews by the authors.

69 Unless otherwise noted, all Glenn Booraem quotations in this chapter are from interviews by the authors.

70 Eric Ries, "The Long-Term Stock Exchange Comes to Life," Medium, October 16, 2017, https://blog.ltse.com/the-long-term-stock-exchange-comes-to-life-c497f29bbc73.

71 Alexander Osipovich and Dennis K. Berman, "Silicon Valley vs. Wall Street: Can the New Long-Term Stock Exchange Disrupt Capitalism?," *Wall Street Journal*, October 16, 2017, https://www.wsj.com/articles/silicon-valley-vs-wall-street-can-the-new-long-term-stock-exchange-disrupt-capitalism-1508151600.

72 Farah Stockman, "Becoming a Steelworker Liberated Her. Then Her Job Moved to Mexico," *New York Times*, October 14, 2017, https://www.nytimes.com/2017/10/14/us/union-jobs-mexico-rexnord.html.

73 Shiva Maniam, "Most Americans See Labor Unions, Corporations Favorably," Pew Research Center, January 30, 2017, http://www.pewresearch.org/fact-tank/2017/01/30/most-americans-see-labor-unions-corporations-favorably/.

74 Umair Irfan, "Tesla's Electric Semi Truck: Elon Musk Unveils His New Freight Vehicle," Vox, November 17, 2017, https://www.vox.com/2017/11/16/16665266/tesla-electric-truck-announced-self-driving-price.

75 American Trucking Association, "Reports, Trends & Statistics," 2018, http://www.trucking.org/News_and_Information_Reports_Industry_Data.aspx.

76 Jonathan Camhi, "Uber to Buy up to 24,000 Volvo SUVs for Self-Driving Fleet," *Business Insider*, November 22, 2017, http://www.businessinsider.com/uber-self-driving-taxi-fleet-24000-new-volvo-suvs-2017-11.

77 Eric Newcomer, "Uber Paid Hackers to Delete Stolen Data on 57 Million People," *Bloomberg Technology*, November 21, 2017, https://www.bloomberg.com/news/articles/2017-11-21/uber-concealed-cyberattack-that-exposed-57-million-people-s-data.

78 McKinsey Global Institute, *A Future That Works: Automation, Employment, and Productivity*, McKinsey & Company, January 2017.

79 United States Census Bureau, "Millennials Outnumber Baby Boomers and Are Far More Diverse, Census Bureau Reports," June 25, 2015, https://www.census.gov/newsroom/press-releases/2015/cb15-113.html.

80 Cited in Andrew Swinand, "Corporate Social Responsibility Is Millennials' New Religion," *Crain's Chicago Business*, March 25, 2014, http://www.chicagobusiness.com/article/20140325/OPINION/140329895/corporate-social-responsibility-is-millennials-new-religion.

81 Bank of America, "Generations Collide as Millennials Redefine Work, Wealth, Family and Influence Finds U.S. Trust 2017 Insights on Wealth and Worth Survey," June 13, 2017, http://www.ustrust.com/publish/content/application/pdf/GWMOL/USTp_WW_2017_Core_News_Release_Final.pdf.

82 Rebecca Darr and Tim Koller, "How to Build an Alliance against Corporate Short-Termism," McKinsey & Company, January 2017.

83 Principles for Responsible Investment, "About the PRI," https://www.unpri.org/about.

84 Unless otherwise noted, all Abe Friedman quotations in this chapter are from interviews by the authors.

85 Diane Cardwell, "Exxon Mobil Shareholders Demand Accounting of Climate Change Policy Risks," May 31, 2017, https://www.nytimes.com/2017/05/31/business/energy-environment/exxon-shareholders-climate-change.html.

Acknowledgments

No book is possible without a special circle of supportive friends and colleagues. First we'd like to thank Steve Kobrin, the executive director of the Wharton Digital Press, and its director and publisher Shannon Berning, who throughout provided strong editorial support, a sharp eye, and ongoing encouragement for this project. Our appreciation also goes to Patti Parker and Wharton Executive Education for their ongoing support. We owe much to our friends at McKinsey, especially Dominic Barton and Rik Kirkland, who helped make this book possible, and Tim Koller, who navigated us through the sometimes choppy waters of corporate finance. Also, McKinsey's Dominique Sanders aided us greatly on the research. We are grateful to Peter Hildick-Smith, who helped us sharpen the focus of our message. And special thanks to Donna Gregor and Liz Frank, who facilitated the CEO contacts interviewed for the book and coordinated the many schedules of four very busy authors with good humor and understanding.

Index

Note: Page numbers in italics refer to figures or tables.

About the Authors

Dennis Carey, a vice chairman of the global executive search firm Korn Ferry, has recruited some of the most successful Fortune 500 CEOs in American business. He is the founder of the CEO Academy, an annual gathering of the nation's top business leaders, and is co-author of five books, including most recently *Boards That Lead* and *Talent Wins: The New Playbook for Putting People First*.

Brian Dumaine is the founder and editor in chief of the New York media company High Water Press and a contributor to *Fortune* magazine, where for three decades he has held various writing and editing positions, including global editor and assistant managing editor. An award-winning journalist, he has produced investigative pieces as well as articles on leadership, investing, technology, and the environment. He is the author of *The Plot to Save the Planet: How Visionary Entrepreneurs and Corporate Titans Are Creating Real Solutions to Global Warming*, and is the editor of the book *The Greatest Business Decisions of All Time*, with a foreword by Jim Collins.

Michael Useem is professor of management, director of the Center for Leadership and Change Management, and faculty director of the McNulty Leadership Program at The Wharton School, University of Pennsylvania. His university teaching includes MBA and executive MBA courses on management and leadership, and he offers programs on leadership and governance for managers in the United States, Asia, Europe, and Latin America. His earlier books include *The Inner Circle, Executive Defense, Investor Capitalism*, and the coauthored *Boards That Lead*.

Rodney Zemmel, the managing partner of McKinsey's New York, Boston, and Stamford offices in the United States, serves clients on growth strategy, performance improvement, and value creation through mergers and acquisitions. He has experience across a range of global industries, with a concentration in healthcare products and services. Beyond healthcare, he leads McKinsey's support for a number of private-equity clients as well as companies in consumer-facing industries.

About Wharton Digital Press

Wharton Digital Press was established to inspire bold, insightful thinking within the global business community. In the tradition of The Wharton School of the University of Pennsylvania and its online business journal, Knowledge@Wharton, Wharton Digital Press uses innovative digital technologies to help managers meet the challenges of today and tomorrow.

As an entrepreneurial publisher, Wharton Digital Press delivers relevant, accessible, conceptually sound, and empirically based business knowledge to readers wherever and whenever they need it. Its format ranges from ebooks to print books available through print-on-demand technology. Directed to a general business audience, the Press's areas of interest include management and strategy, innovation and entrepreneurship, finance and investment, leadership, marketing, operations, human resources, social responsibility, and business–government relations.

http://wdp.wharton.upenn.edu/

About The Wharton School

Founded in 1881 as the first collegiate business school, The Wharton School of the University of Pennsylvania is recognized globally for intellectual leadership and ongoing innovation across every major discipline of business education. With a broad global community and one of the most published business school faculties, Wharton creates economic and social value around the world. The School has 5,000 undergraduate, MBA, executive MBA, and doctoral students; more than 9,000 participants in executive education programs annually; and a powerful alumni network of 96,000 graduates.

http://wdp.wharton.upenn.edu/